NORTH OF BIRMINGHAM

Vic Mitchell

MP Middleton Press

Front cover: A train of diesel locomotives has just run over Bescot Junction; the Pleck Curve to Walsall is behind the rear engine. The class 47s are between the platforms of Bescot station on 19th November 1983. (Colour-Rail.com)

*Back cover upper: Steam was resurrected in the area by the Chasewater Railway and Bagnall 0-4-0ST no. 2648 **Linda** of 1940 was in action at Brownhills West on 20th March 2011. The 40-lever signal box had been in use at Madeley, south of Crewe, from 1930 to 2004. (J.Whitehouse)*

Back cover lower: No. 47423 is at Water Orton East Junction. The wartime signal box was built with a concrete roof, impervious to the majority of bombs, but this was a latecomer of similar style, built in 1963. (Colour-Rail.com)

Published February 2014

ISBN 978 1 908174 55 0

© Middleton Press, 2014

Design Deborah Esher
Typesetting Barbara Mitchell

Published by
    Middleton Press
    Easebourne Lane
    Midhurst
    West Sussex
    GU29 9AZ
Tel: 01730 813169
Fax: 01730 812601
Email: info@middletonpress.co.uk
www.middletonpress.co.uk

Printed in the United Kingdom by Henry Ling Limited, at the Dorset Press, Dorchester, DT1 1HD

CONTENTS

INDEX

ACKNOWLEDGEMENTS

I am very grateful for the assistance received from many of those mentioned in the credits, also to A.R.Carder, A.J.Castledine, G.Croughton, S.Davies, S.C.Jenkins, N.Langridge, Mr D. and Dr S.Salter, T.Walsh and in particular Barbara Mitchell, my ever caring wife.

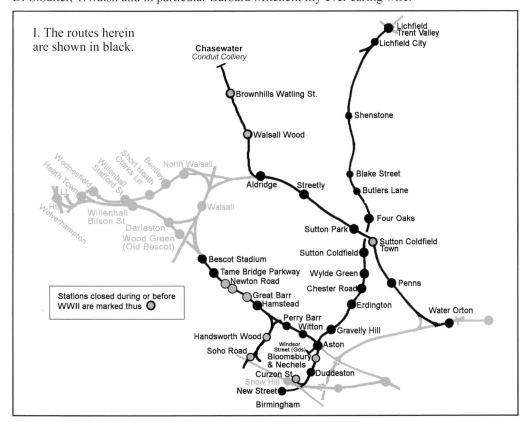

GEOGRAPHICAL SETTING

The southern part of the area covered by this album was within the Black Country, a term used as a result of the industrial revolution. The presence of coal, iron ore and fire clays near the surface resulted in intensive workings and widespread pollution of the atmosphere and the landscape. The transport demands of the industries resulted in an extensive network of canals in this part of the Midland Plain, most of the waterways still remaining complete, despite the arrival of competing railways.

A number of brooks drain the area, mostly into the River Tame, which flows east, north of Birmngham and then curves north to Tamworth. In addition to the valuable minerals mentioned, the district has extensive deposits of red sandstone and marl. The eastern lines were built in south Staffordshire, the remainder being in Warwickshire.

Birmingham became Britain's second largest city and its most important manufacturing centre. It incorporated the market town of Sutton Coldfield in 1974, when many boundary changes took place.

The maps are to the scale of 25ins to 1 mile with north at the top, unless otherwise indicated.

HISTORICAL BACKGROUND

The London & Birmingham Railway completed its line north to Curzon Street in 1837-38 and the Grand Junction Railway aimed to link it with Manchester, although bypassing Wolverhampton. It opened between Birmingham (Vauxhall) and Warrington on 4th July 1837. The route via Birmingham (New Street) and Wolverhampton was not completed until 1854. These lines all became part of the London & North Western Railway in 1846.

The Birmingham & Derby Junction Railway opened through Water Orton in 1842 and became part of the Midland Railway in 1844. Its line through Sutton Coldfield to Wolverhampton opened as far as North Walsall on 1st July 1879. It then ran to Wolverhampton, using the 1872 tracks of the Wolverhampton & Walsall Railway. The MR ran north from Aldridge to Brownhills from 1st July 1884, its branch having been used for coal traffic two years earlier. Passenger traffic ceased on it on 31st March 1930.

The Birmingham to Sutton Coldfield section was brought into use by the LNWR on 2nd June 1862 and was extended north to Lichfield on 15th December 1884. Here it met the 1847 LNWR route between Rugby and Stafford, plus the 1849 line of the South Staffordshire Railway from Walsall.

The short link line through Handsworth Wood and Soho Road came into use in 1887, but only carried passengers between 1st April 1889 and 5th May 1941. It was part of the LNWR. This and the MR became constituents of the London Midland & Scottish Railway in the Grouping of 1923. Closures to goods traffic are noted in the captions.

Privatisation brought Central Trains to run local services from 2nd March 1997 and London Midland took them over on 11th November 2007.

Much fresh historical data has come to light recently and so some facts will differ from earlier publications.

Electrification

Birmingham-Bescot-Walsall services were electrically operated from 6th March 1967 and extension to Rugeley was announced for 2015. The line from Birmingham to Lichfield had electric trains from 12th July 1993.

PASSENGER SERVICES

The complex route layouts of the area have made the choice of album coverage difficult, so this has been primarily geographic and not operational, thus the selection of timetables to illustrate services cannot match the routes precisely. Therefore the extracts have been placed near the start of each of the three sections of this volume and they inevitably cover a greater distance, but indicate destinations.

The sample frequencies are evident and so are not listed. Recent regular interval services are mentioned, but not generally reproduced in tables, owing to their length.

The Brownhills Branch: two extracts are shown below the first two main line tables, although one is headed "Walsall-Wood Branch". It seems that provision was made for a Saturday night out, albeit of somewhat limited duration.

September 1885

BIRMINGHAM, SUTTON COLDFIELD, WALSALL, and WOLVERHAMPTON.

	mrn	mrn	mrn	mrn	mrn	mrn	mrn	aft	mrn	mrn	non	aft	aft	aft	aft	aft	aft	aft	Sundays.				
Wellington Sta.,																							
Leeds 235....dep	20 20	2 20	2 20	....	8 20	8 50	....	....	1145	....	1 25	....	....	3 15	4 35	....	6 20	....	2 20	....	....	7 0
Derby 246.. "	4 57	6 29	6 45	8 45	1032	1140	....	....	2 5	....	3 45	....	....	5 35	7 5	....	9 0	....	6 35	....	....	2 15
London (St.P.) "	....	....	....	5 15	....	8 10	....	10 5	....	12 0	1225 k	....	3 40	....	....	....	....	....	....	....	....
Leicester 254 "	....	....	....	8 10	....	1125	....	1235	....	2 20	3 32	....	5 40	....	6 52	....	....	mrn	mrn	aft	aft	aft
Birmingham (N.S) d	7 58	0 9	5	....	1122	....	1 20	1 55	3 5	....	4 58	6 18	....	7 10	8 25	....	1055	....	9 30	....	2 30	7 30
Saltley	7 10	8	6 9	10	....	1128	....	1 25	2 0	3 10	....	5 3	6 23	....	7 15	8 30	....	11 0	....	9 36	....	2 36	7 36
Castle Bromwich	....	....	9 19	....	1138	....	1 34	Sat.	3 20	....	5 13	6 32	....	7 25	8 40	....	11 8	....	....	....	....	....
Water Orton dep	....	....	10 2	....	1245	....	....	....	3 44	....	....	6 43	....	....	....	....	1118	....	....	....	....
Penns	....	8 18	9 27	b	1146	....	1 42	2 14	3 28	d	5 21	6 40	6 50	7 33	8 48	....	1125	....	9 48	....	2 48	7 43
Sutton Coldfield *	7 26	8 23	9 32	1011	1151	1255	1 47	2 19	3 33	3 53	5 26	6 45	6 56	7 38	8 53	....	1130	....	9 53	....	2 53	7 53
Sutton Park	7 29	8 26	9 35	b	1154	1257	1 50	2 22	3 36	b	5 29	6 48	6 59	7 41	8 56	....	....	....	9 56	....	2 56	7 56
Streetly	7 35	8 32	9 41	b	12 0	c	1 56	2 25	3 42	d	5 35	6 54	7 5	7 47	9 2	....	....	....	10 2	....	3 2	8 2
Aldridge (see side)	7 40	8 37	9 46	b	12 5	1 8	2 1	2 33	3 47	b	5 40	6 59	7 12	7 52	9 7	....	1138	....	10 7	....	3 7	8 7
Walsall {arr	7 48	8 45	9 55	1026	1213	1 16	2 9	2 41	3 55	4 8	5 48	7 8	7 18	8 0	9 15	....	1116	....	1015	....	3 15	8 15
{dep	6 47	7 53	9 0	1029	1217	1 22	....	2 48	....	4 18	5 51	....	7 21	....	9 30	1045	....	8 30	....	2 0	....	8 27
North Walsall	6 52	....	9 5	1034	1222	....	....	2 53	....	4 23	5 56	....	7 26	....	....	....	....	8 35	....	2 5	....	8 32
Bentley....(Lane)	7 59	....	....	....	1226	....	....	2 57	....	....	6 0	....	Sat.	....	....	....	....	....	....	....	....	....
Short Heath (Clark's)	....	....	9 10	....	1230	....	....	3 1	....	....	6 4	....	7 31	....	....	....	....	8 40	....	2 10	....	8 37
Willenhall (Market	6 58	8	4 9 13	....	1040	1233	1 31	....	3 4	4 29	....	6 7	....	7 34	....	9 39	1054	....	8 43	....	2 13	....	8 40
Wednesfield (Place)	7 3	8	9 9 18	....	1045	1238	1 36	....	3 9	4 34	....	6 12	....	7 39	....	9 44	1059	....	8 48	....	2 18	....	8 45
Heath Town	7 6	....	9 21	....	1048	1242	m	....	3 12	....	....	6 15	....	7 42	....	....	....	....	8 51	....	2 21	....	8 48
Wolverhampton ar	7 11	8 13	9 26	....	1052	1245	1 40	....	3 17	4 38	....	6 20	....	7 47	....	9 48	11 3	....	8 56	....	2 26	....	8 53
Wolverhampton dp	....	7 22	....	....	8 23	1022	....	1214	1 15	....	....	3 50	5 20	6 30	7 50	8 50	1035	1115	9 15	2 40	....	9 5
Heath Town	....	....	....	....	8 27	1026	....	....	1 19	....	....	6 34	7 54	8 53	....	....	....	9 19	2 44	....	9 9
Wednesfield (Place)	....	7 27	....	....	8 31	1030	....	1219	1 23	....	....	3 55	5 25	6 38	7 58	8 57	1040	1120	9 23	2 48	....	9 13
Willenhall (Market	....	7 31	....	....	8 36	1034	....	1224	1 28	....	....	3 59	5 30	6 43	8 3	9 2	1045	1125	9 28	2 53	....	9 18
Short Heath (Clark's	....	....	....	....	8 39	....	....	....	1 31	....	....	i	....	6 46	8 6	....	....	....	9 31	2 56	....	9 21
Bentley......(Lane)	....	....	....	....	8 43	....	....	....	1 35	....	....	....	6 50	....	....	....	....	....	....	....	....
North Walsall	....	7 38	....	....	8 46	1040	....	....	1 38	....	....	4 5	....	6 53	8 10	....	....	1130	9 35	3 0	....	9 25
Walsall {arr	....	7 42	....	....	8 52	1046	....	1232	1 44	....	....	4 11	5 58	7 0	8 16	9 10	1053	1138	9 41	3 6	....	9 31
{dep	6 45	7 45	7 50	8 20	8 56	1050	11 5	1235	1 47	2 25	3 37	4 15	5 58	7 0	8 16	9 10	1053	1138	9 41	3 6	....	9 31
Aldridge (see side)	6 52	a	7 57	8 27	9 3	g	1112	1242	1 54	e	g 3 44	4 22	5 49	7 16	8 27	9 53	....	....	9 55	3 19	8 49	....
Streetly	....	7 55	....	8 33	....	h	1118	1248	2 0	....	3 50	h	5 55	7 22	8 33	Sat.	....	....	10 13	3 25	8 55	....
Sutton Park	....	a	8	8 39	9 11	11 4	1123	1253	2 5	2 40	3 55	4 31	6 0	7 27	8 38	10 2	....	....	10 7	3 31	9 1	....
Sutton Coldfield *	7 1	8 1	8	8 41	9 15	11 6	1127	1257	2 9	2 48	3 59	4 36	4 7	7 31	8 42	10 4	....	....	10 9	3 33	9 3	....
Penns 254	7 6	a	8 13	8 46	9 20	1	1132	1 2	2 14	....	4 4	....	6 9	7 36	8 47	10 9	....	....	1014	3 38	9 8	....
Water Ortn 249.	....	8 10	....	....	1116	....	....	....	2 52	....	4 44	....	....	....	....	....	....	....	....	....
Castle Bromwich	7 14	....	....	8 54	....	f	2 22	....	4 12	....	6 17	....	....	1017	....	....	....	....	....
Saltley 246, 249, 250	7 20	....	8 59	0 9	34	....	1143	1 12	2 23	....	4 18	....	6 23	7 47	8 50	1023	....	....	1024	3 48	9 18
Birmingham (N.S) a	7 27	....	8 33	9 10	9 42	....	1152	1 20	2 35	....	4 25	....	6 30	7 53	9 5	1030	....	....	1030	3 55	9 25
Leicester 254 ar	9 5	9 22	....	....	1224	....	....	4 15	4 15	....	5 55	8 12	....	....	1 42	....	....	7 15	1 42
London (St.P.) "	....	1150	....	....	8 15	....	....	7 15	7 15	....	8 15	2 20	....	....	4 15	....	....	9 45	4 15
Derby 249.... "	9 12	9 22	....	1010	....	1232	1250	2 35	3 36	5 23	6 0	6 0	7 50	9 55	....	1140	....	....	6 5	1238
Leeds 235 .... "	12 0	12 0	....	1 0	....	3 20	5 22	6 0	....	9 5	9 5	1038	....	2 15	....	....	10 0	3 0

Notes

a Stops when required to take up for Leicester and Stations beyond; also for Burton and places North thereof. **b** Stop to set down from Stations beyond Water Orton, on informing Guard at preceding *stopping* Station. **c** Stops to set down from Burton or Stations North thereof on informing Guard at Sutton Park. **d** Stops to set down from London on informing Guard at preceding *stopping* Station. **e** Stops on Saturdays. **g** Stop when required to take up for Leicester, Derby, and Stations beyond. **h** Stop when required to take up for Burton or Stations North thereof, or for London.

WALSALL-WOOD BRANCH.

	mrn	aft	aft	aft
Brownhills	8 5	1 35	6 55	8 50
Walsall-W.	8 11	1 41	7 1	8 56
Aldridge	8 17	1 47	7 7	9 2
Aldridge d	8 42	2 7	7 22	10 0
Walsall-W.	8 49	2 14	7 29	10 8
Brownhills	8 55	2 20	7 35	1015

BIRMINGHAM, CASTLE BROMWICH, WALSALL, and WOLVERHAMPTON.—L. M. & S.

Miles from Birmingham		Week Days.																		Sundays.		
		mrn	mrn	mrn	mrn		aft	mrn	aft	aft	aft	aft		aft	aft	aft	aft	aft		mrn	mrn	non
	546 Leeds (Wellington) dep	....	....	3 6	....	....	....	8 15	12b42		....	12b42	....	2 45	3 30	5 22	....	5 55	....	....	3 6	12 0
	556 Derby .... "	....	....	6 38	9 5	....	....	1155	2 56	Except Saturdays.	....	3 36	....	5 5	6 0	7 45	....	9 2	....	....	6 35	2 55
	604 Leicester (Lon. Rd.) "	....	....	6 30	8 22	....	....	11 7	2 10		....	4 5	....	....	5 45	7 22	....	....	....	....	....	....
—	Birmingham (New St.) dep	....	7 24	8 15	1050	....	....	1 12	4 6		....	5 35	....	6 32	7 15	9 8	....	1047	....	....	9 25	7 30
2	Saltley	....	7 30	8 21	1057	....	....	1 17	4 12		....	5 41	....	6 38	7 22	9 15	....	1052	....	....	9 30	7 36
5¼	Castle Bromwich	....	7 36	8 27	11 3	....	....	1 25	4 18		....	5 47	....	6 44	7 28	9 21	....	1059	....	....	....	....
8½	Penns	....	7 46	8 35	1111	....	....	1 33	4 26		....	5 55	....	6 52	7 36	9 29	....	11 7	....	....	9 43	7 47
11	Sutton Park	6 43	7 56	8 41	1117	....	1 21	1 42	4 32	5 22	....	6 1	....	6 58	7 45	9 35	....	1113	....	....	9 49	7 53
13¼	Streetly	6 49	8 2	8 47	1123	....	1 27	1 48	4 38	5 28	....	6 7	....	7 4	7 53	9 41	....	1119	....	....	9 55	7 59
15¾	Aldridge *(below)*	6 54	8 7	8 52	1128	....	1 32	1 53	4 43	5 33	....	6 12	....	7 9	7 59	9 46	....	1124	....	....	10 0	8 4
17¼	Walsall .... arr.	7 2	8 18	9 1	1137	....	1 41	2 2	4 54	5 41	....	6 23	....	7 19	8 10	9 54	....	1132	....	....	1010	8 12
	Walsall .... dep.	7 13	8 30	9 13	1141	....	1 46	2 15	5 27	....	6 17	6 36	....	7 53	8 20	9 58	1036	....	....	8 42	1017	8 19
21	ShortHeath (Clark's Lane)	....	8 41	....	....	....	....	2 26	....	....	6 28	....	....	....	....	....	....	....	....	....	....	....
21¾	Willenhall (Stafford St.)..	....	8 50	....	....	....	....	2 29	....	....	6 31	....	....	....	....	....	....	....	....	8 54	1030	8 32
18¾	Pleck	7 15	....	9 15	1143	....	1 48	....	5 29	....	....	6 38	....	7 55	8 22	10 0	1038	....	....	....	....	....
19¾	Darlaston	7 18	....	9 19	1147	....	1 52	....	5 33	....	....	6 41	....	7 59	8 26	10 4	1042	....	....	....	....	....
21¼	Willenhall (Bilston St.).	7 22	....	9 23	1151	....	1 56	....	5 37	....	....	6 45	....	8 5	8 30	10 8	1046	....	....	....	....	....
23	Wednesfield	....	8 54	....	....	....	....	2 33	....	....	6 35	....	....	....	....	....	....	....	....	....	....	....
24½	Wolverhampton ..... arr.	7 31	9 1	9 33	12 1	....	2 5	2 38	5 47	....	6 40	6 59	....	8 14	8 40	1020	1058	....	....	9 2	1037	8 39

Miles		Week Days.																		Sundays.		
		mrn	mrn	mrn	mrn	mrn	mrn		aft	aft	aft	aft	aft	aft	aft	aft	aft	aft		mrn	mrn	aft
	Wolverhampton ..... dep	....	5 56	7 20	8 22	9 28	9 50	....	1215	1241	1 31	3 45	5 15	5 28	6 29	7 34	8 0	9 4	....	9 38	1055	9 4
1¾	Wednesfield	....	....	....	....	....	9 57	....	1222	....	....	....	....	....	6 36	....	8 7	....	....	....	....	....
3	Willenhall (Bilston St.).	....	6 3	7 26	8 29	9 36	....	....	....	1249	1 37	3 52	5 24	5 35	....	7 42	....	9 15	....	....	....	....
4¾	Darlaston	....	6 7	7 30	8 33	9 42	....	....	....	1254	1 41	3 56	5 29	5 39	....	7 47	....	9 22	....	....	....	....
5½	Pleck	....	6 10	7 33	8 36	9 46	....	....	....	1257	1 45	3 59	5 33	5 42	....	7 50	....	9 24	....	....	....	....
3	Willenhall (Stafford St.)..	....	....	....	....	....	10 2	....	1227	....	....	....	....	....	6 42	....	8 12	....	....	9 46	11 4	9 12
3¾	ShortHeath (Clark's Lane)	....	....	....	....	....	10 6	....	1231	....	....	....	....	....	6 48	....	....	....	....	....	....	....
7¼	Walsall .... arr.	....	6 15	7 36	8 41	9 51	1017	....	1242	1 2	1 50	4 4	5 37	5 47	6 59	7 55	8 24	9 29	....	9 59	1117	9 25
	Walsall .... dep.	6 12	7 5	8 10	9 1	10 8	....	....	1250	1 22	2 34	4 18	5 43	6 33	....	8 2	....	9 50	....	....	1124	9 32
9	Aldridge *(below)*	6 20	7 13	8 21	9 9	10 16	....	....	1258	1 30	2 42	4 26	5 53	6 42	....	8 10	....	9 58	....	....	1132	9 40
11¼	Streetly	6 25	7 18	8 27	9 14	10 21	....	....	1 3	1 35	2 47	4 31	5 58	6 47	....	8 15	....	10 3	....	....	1137	9 45
13¾	Sutton Park	6 29	7 23	8 32	9 19	10 26	....	....	1 7	1 40	2 52	4 35	6 3	6 52	....	8 20	....	10 9	....	....	1142	9 50
16	Penns	....	7 29	8 38	9 25	10 32	....	....	....	1 46	2 58		6 9	6 58	....	8 27	....	1015	....	....	1148	9 56
19¼	Castle Bromwich 560, 605	....	7d39	8 45	9 32	10 39	....	....	....	1 53	3 6	Except Saturdays.	6h20	7 6	....	8 34	....	1022	....	....	....	....
22¾	Saltley 560, 605.. | 605, 620	....	7 48	8 54	9 41	10 47	....	....	....	2 1	3 15		6 28	7 15	....	8 43	....	1030	....	....	12 0	10 8
24¾	Birmingham A 369, arr.	....	7 55	9 0	9 47	10 53	....	....	....	2 7	3 21		6 35	7 21	....	8 49	....	1037	....	....	12 6	1014
64¾	605 Leicester (L. Rd.) arr.	....	8 46	1039	....	12 20	....	....	....	3 4	5 58		....	9 0	....	....	....	1l35	....	....	2p42	2p0
65¾	560 Derby .... "	....	9 26	9 57	1118	12 40	....	....	....	4 0	5 28		8 8	....	....	1028	....	1215	....	....	1 21	1215
141¾	537 Leeds (Wellington) "		e1130	1238	1 19	3 4	....	....	....	5 58	7 58		1045	....	....	1 42	....	3 27	....	....	4 17	3 27

A New Street; about ¼ mile to Moor Street and about ⅓ mile to Snow Hill Stations.
b Passengers can depart Leeds at 12 55 aft., changing at Chesterfield. *d* Arrives at 7 35 mrn. *e* Except Saturdays.
h Arrives 6 15 aft. *l* Via Derby. Arrives at 12 10 mrn. on Sundays. *p* Via Derby.

BROWNHILLS and ALDRIDGE.—L. M. & S.

Miles		Week Days only.						
		mrn		aft S		aft E		
—	Brownhills (Watling St.) dep.	7 52	....	4 20	....	5 57	....	....
2	Walsall Wood	7 59	....	4 27	....	6 4	....	....
4	Aldridge *(above)* .... arr.	8 6	....	4 34	....	6 11	....	....

Miles		Week Days only.					
		mrn		aft E		aft S	
—	Aldridge .... dep.	8 30	....	6 45	....	8 13	....
2	Walsall Wood	8 38	....	6 53	....	8 21	....
4	Brownhills B 378 .. arr.	8 45	....	7 0	....	8 28	....

B Watling Street Station; ½ mile to Brownhills (High Street Station). **E** Except Saturdays. **S** Saturdays only.

September 1925

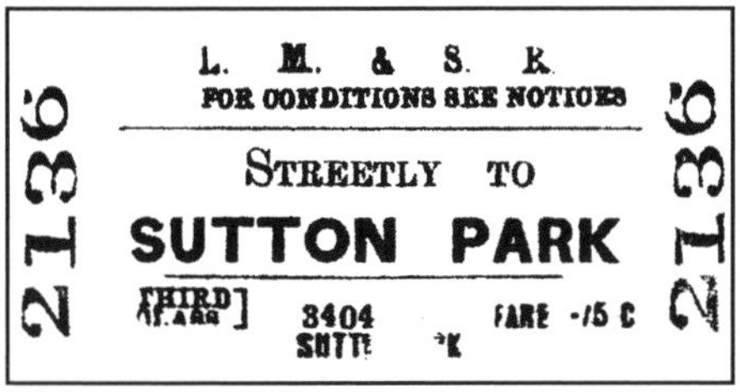

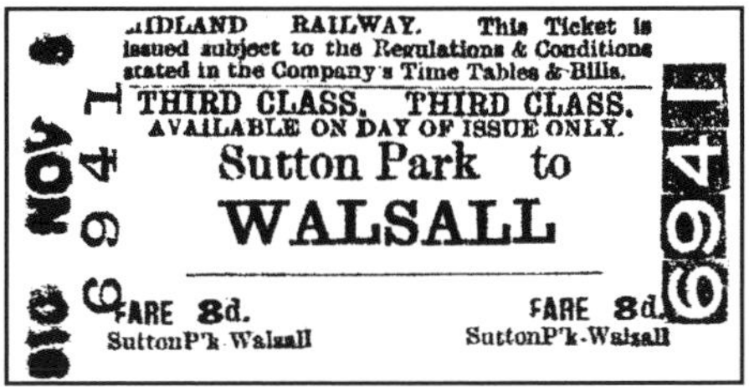

BIRMINGHAM, CASTLE BROMWICH, and WALSALL.

Miles	Week Days only	mrn	mrn		aft	aft	aft	aft	
—	Birmingham (NewSt) dep	7 18	8 13	..	1 10	5 35	6 35	8 5	..
2	Saltley	7 24	8 19	..	1 16	5 41	6 41	8 12	..
5¼	Castle Bromwich	7 30	8 25	..	1 22	5 47	6 47	8 19	..
8¾	Penns, for Walmley	7 37	8 32	..	1 29	5 54	6 54	..	..
10	Sutton Park	7 4	8 38	..	1 35	6 0	7 0	8 29	..
13¼	Streetly	7 52	8 44	..	1 41	6 6	7 6	8 35	..
15¾	Aldridge	7 58	8 50	..	1 47	6 12	7 12	8 41	..
17¾	Walsall arr.	8 4	8 56	..	1 53	6 18	7 18	8 47	..

Miles	Week Days only	mrn	mrn		aft	aft	aft	
—	Walsall dep.	7 0	8 10	..	1 36	5 43	6 40	..
1¼	Aldridge	7 9	8 17	..	1 43	5 50	6 47	..
4½	Streetly	7 15	8 22	..	1 48	5 55	6 52	..
7½	Sutton Park	7 23	8 27	..	1 55	6 3	6 57	..
8½	Penns, for Walmley	7 31	8 33	..	2 3	6 12	7 3	..
12¼	Castle Bromwich 660, 688	7 37	8 39	..	2 9	6 20	7 12	..
15½	Saltley [724	7 45	8 46	..	2 15	6 28	7 21	..
17½	Birmingham A 475, arr.	7 51	8 52	..	2 22	6 35	7 29	..

A NewStreet

May 1944

December 1957

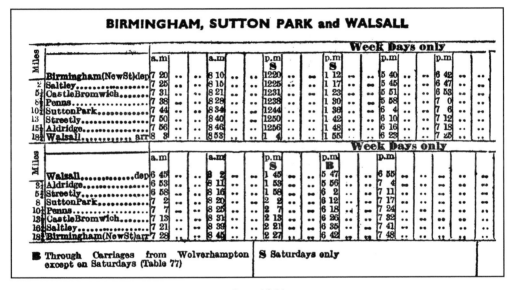

BIRMINGHAM, SUTTON PARK and WALSALL

Miles	Week Days only	a.m			a.m			p.m S			p.m S			p.m			p.m		
	Birmingham (NewSt) dep	7 20	..	..	8 10	..	..	1220	..	..	1 12	..	..	5 40	..	..	6 42	..	..
2	Saltley	7 25	..	..	8 15	..	..	1225	..	..	1 17	..	..	5 45	..	..	6 47	..	..
5¼	CastleBromwich	7 31	..	..	8 21	..	..	1231	..	..	1 23	..	..	5 51	..	..	6 53	..	..
8¼	Penns	7 38	..	..	8 28	..	..	1238	..	..	1 30	..	..	5 58	..	..	7 0	..	..
10¾	SuttonPark	7 44	..	..	8 34	..	..	1244	..	..	1 36	..	..	6 4	..	..	7 6	..	..
13	Streetly	7 50	..	..	8 40	..	..	1250	..	..	1 42	..	..	6 10	..	..	7 12	..	..
15½	Aldridge	7 56	..	..	8 46	..	..	1256	..	..	1 48	..	..	6 16	..	..	7 18	..	..
18¾	Walsall arr	8 3	..	..	8 53	..	..	1 4	..	..	1 55	..	..	6 23	..	..	7 25	..	..

Miles	Week Days only	a.m			a.m			p.m S			p.m B			p.m					
	Walsall dep	6 45	..	..	8 2	..	..	1 45	..	..	5 47	..	..	6 55	..	..	..	..	..
3¼	Aldridge	6 53	..	..	8 11	..	..	1 53	..	..	5 56	..	..	7 4	..	..	..	..	..
5¾	Streetly	6 58	..	..	8 16	..	..	1 58	..	..	6 2	..	..	7 11	..	..	..	..	..
8	SuttonPark	7 2	..	..	8 20	..	..	2 2	..	..	6 12	..	..	7 17	..	..	..	..	..
10½	Penns	7 7	..	..	8 25	..	..	2 7	..	..	6 18	..	..	7 24	..	..	..	..	..
13½	CastleBromwich	7 13	..	..	8 31	..	..	2 13	..	..	6 26	..	..	7 32	..	..	..	..	..
16½	Saltley	7 21	..	..	8 39	..	..	2 21	..	..	6 35	..	..	7 41	..	..	..	..	..
18¾	Birmingham (NewSt) arr	7 28	..	..	8 45	..	..	2 27	..	..	6 42	..	..	7 48	..	..	..	..	..

B Through Carriages from Wolverhampton except on Saturdays (Table 77)

S Saturdays only

June 1964

BIRMINGHAM, SUTTON PARK AND WALSALL

Miles		WEEKDAYS										SUNDAYS							
						SO	SX												
		a.m.		a.m.		p.m.	p.m.		p.m.		p.m.	p.m.	p.m.	p.m.	p.m.	p.m.	p.m.	p.m.	p.m.
0	BIRMINGHAM New St. dep.	7 15	.	8 5	.	12 20	1 10	.	5 40	.	6 49	.	.	.	.	.	.	.	.
2	Saltley	7 19	...	8 9	...	12 24	1 14	...	5 44	...	6 53	...	...	...	...	...	...	...	...
5¼	Castle Bromwich	7 24	.	8 14	.	12 29	1 19	.	5 49	.	6 58	.	.	.	.	.	.	.	.
8¼	Penns	7 31	...	8 21	...	12 36	1 26	...	5 56	...	7 5	...	...	...	...	...	...	...	...
11	Sutton Park	7 37	.	8 27	.	12 42	1 32	.	6 2	.	7 11	2 45	3 45	4 45	5 45	6 45	7 45	8 45	9 45
13½	Streetly	7 43	...	8 32	...	12 47	1 37	...	6 7	...	7 16	2 49	3 49	4 49	5 49	6 49	7 49	8 49	9 49
15¾	Aldridge	7 48	.	8 37	.	12 52	1 42	.	6 12	.	7 21	2 54	3 54	4 54	5 54	6 54	7 54	8 54	9 54
19	WALSALL arr.	7 56	...	8 45	.	12 59	1 49	...	6 19	...	7 28	3 2	4 2	5 2	6 2	7 2	8 2	9 2	10 2

Miles		WEEKDAYS										SUNDAYS							
		SO	SX	SX	SO	SO		SX											
		a.m.	a.m.	a.m.	a.m.	p.m.		p.m.	p.m.		p.m.	p.m.	p.m.	p.m.	p.m.	p.m.	p.m.	p.m.	p.m.
0	WALSALL dep.	6A35	6 45	8 8	8 0	1 46	.	2 16	5 53	.	6 54	2 15	3 15	4 15	5 15	6 15	7 15	8 15	9 15
3¼	Aldridge	6 43	6 54	8 8	8 8	1 53	...	2 23	6 1	...	7 1	2 22	3 22	4 22	5 22	6 22	7 22	8 22	9 22
5¾	Streetly	6 49	6 58	8 13	8 13	1 57	.	2 27	6 6	.	7 5	2 26	3 26	4 26	5 26	6 26	7 26	8 26	9 26
8	Sutton Park	6 54	7 2	8 17	8 17	2 0	...	2 32	6 10	...	7 10	2 31	3 31	4 31	5 31	6 31	7 31	8 31	9 31
10½	Penns	7 0	7 7	8 22	8 22	2 6	.	2 36	6 15	.	7 14	.	.	.	.	.	.	.	.
13¾	Castle Bromwich	7 9	7 13	8 28	8 28	2 13	...	2 44	6 24	...	7 21	...	...	...	...	...	...	...	...
17	Saltley	7 19	7 21	8 35	8 37	2 21	.	2 52	6 32	.	7 29	.	.	.	.	.	.	.	.
19	BIRMINGHAM New St. arr.	7 25	7 28	8 40	8 42	2 27	...	2 58	6 39	...	7 35	...	...	...	...	...	...	...	...

A—Through Carriages to Kingswear arr. 1.50 p.m. SO—Saturdays only. SX—Saturdays excepted.

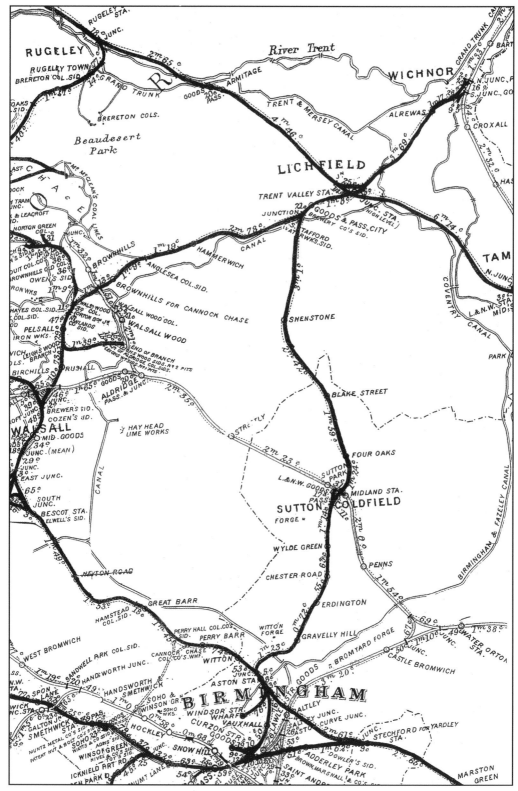

II.   Airey's map of 1887 has the MR route with an open line, running across the map. This is the subject of Section 1 and the part to become the Chasewater Railway is north of Brownhills and is semi-circular. The scale is 2 miles to 1 inch.

1. Chasewater to Water Orton
CONDUIT COLLIERY

1.   Conduit No. 3 Colliery was often referred to as "Jerome's" and we are looking south along the LNWR Five Ways branch in about 1905, towards Conduit Junction. The Midland Railway was served from the colliery by a line which left the colliery from the left of the picture and curved northwards, before completing a half-circle to Conduit Colliery Sidings, at the end of the MR line. This connection was retained for use by colliery locomotives travelling between Five Ways Colliery and the Chasetown NCB workshops, locally known as "Wembley". This use, in part, contributed to a section of the MR line being saved to become part of the Chasewater Railway. (HMRS)

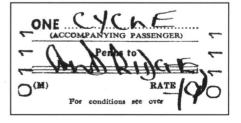

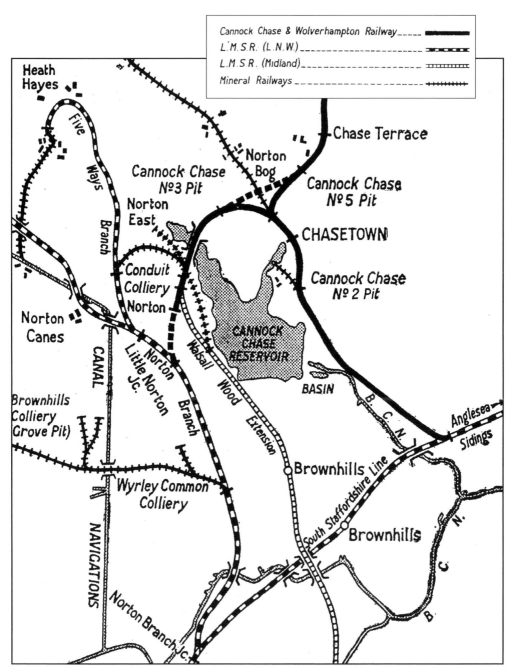

Legend:
- Cannock Chase & Wolverhampton Railway
- L.M.S.R. (L.N.W.)
- L.M.S.R. (Midland)
- Mineral Railways

Heath Hayes

Five Ways Branch

Cannock Chase Nº3 Pit

Norton Bog

Chase Terrace

Cannock Chase Nº 5 Pit

CHASETOWN

Norton East

Conduit Colliery Norton

Cannock Chase Nº 2 Pit

Norton Canes

CANAL

Little Norton Jc.

Norton Branch

Walsall Wood Extension

CANNOCK CHASE RESERVOIR

BASIN

B.C.N.

Anglesea Sidings

Brownhills Colliery (Grove Pit)

Wyrley Common Colliery

Brownhills

South Staffordshire Line

Brownhills

B.C.N.

NAVIGATIONS

Norton Branch Jc.

IIIa. 1947 diagram. BCN refers to the Birmingham Canal Navigation.
The area is on the left of the previous map. (The Railway Magazine).

CHASEWATER RAILWAY

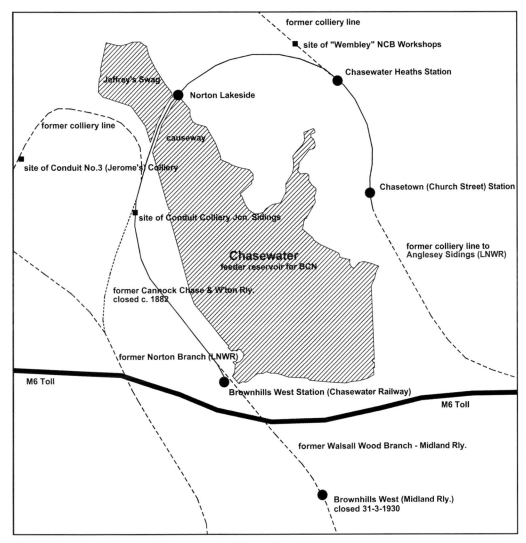

former colliery line

site of "Wembley" NCB Workshops

Chasewater Heaths Station

Jeffrey's Swag

Norton Lakeside

former colliery line

causeway

site of Conduit No.3 (Jerome's) Colliery

Chasetown (Church Street) Station

site of Conduit Colliery Jcn. Sidings

Chasewater
feeder reservoir for BCN

former colliery line to
Anglesey Sidings (LNWR)

former Cannock Chase & W'ton Rly.
closed c. 1882

former Norton Branch (LNWR)

M6 Toll

Brownhills West Station (Chasewater Railway)

M6 Toll

former Walsall Wood Branch - Midland Rly.

Brownhills West (Midland Rly.)
closed 31-3-1930

IIIb. A group of preservationists met in November 1959 and began to collect historic rolling stock in a siding at Hednesford. A country park was begun by the local authority on land adjacent to Chasewater Reservoir. This had been created in the 1770s to supply water to the Wyrley & Essington Canal. On its west bank had been a colliery railway owned by the MR. The trackbed of this 1881 line was leased to the group in 1964 and it became the Chasewater Light Railway Society in 1973. Having relaid much track, occasional public steamings were held until October 1982. The original terminus was swallowed up by the M6, however this allowed for the development of a new station. The Chasewater Light Railway & Museum Company was formed in 1985 and regular operation from Brownhills West followed. Known as "The Colliery Line", extension from Chasewater Heaths to Chasetown (Church Street) took place on 7th March 2004. The route from Brownhills West thus became almost two miles long and its popularity grew. Route diagram in 2013. (I.Pell)

2.   Standing at Brownhills West on 9th December 2009 is *Linda*, a Bagnall 0-4-0ST built in 1940. The roof on the right is on the six-road shed, which was completed in 2004. A 2ft gauge demonstration line carried passengers from 12th September 2010. On site in 2013 were four DMU cars, ten steam and 12 diesel locomotives. (J.Whitehouse)

Opening times can be found on
www.chasewaterrailway.com or telephone **01543 452623.**

IV. Brownhills West track layout in 2013. (I.Pell)

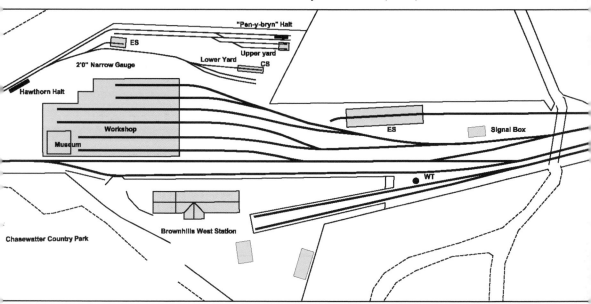

3.   Norton Lakeside, as the name implies, is located near to Norton Pool. Today, these waters are better known as Chasewater, which is how the railway gained its name. In 2013 the dam at the end of this feeder reservoir to the Wyrley & Essington Canal was completely repaired after years of decline. South of the station the line is carried on a causeway over part of the Pool; the causeway was restored from 1993 onwards and Norton Lakeside opened in December 1995. The Wildfowl Reserve is adjacent to it. (I.Pell)

4. Chasewater Heaths was photographed on 18th March 2012 with *Nechells No.4*, a Robert Stephenson & Hawthorn 0-6-0T. The station building was started in June 1999 and completed in April 2000. The signal box arrived in 2007, from Hademore Crossing, south of Lichfield. (J.Whitehouse)

5. Chasetown (Church Street) is the end of the line and consists of a basic single platform with run round facilities. There are no station buildings and it is unlikely that the line will proceed further, as beyond the buffer stop is Chasetown Rugby Club! The station was the last to be opened on the Chasewater Railway in 2004 and is seen on 13th October 2013, with Andrew Barclay 0-4-0ST no. 1223 *Colin McAndrew* of 1911. (I.Pell)

BROWNHILLS WATLING STREET

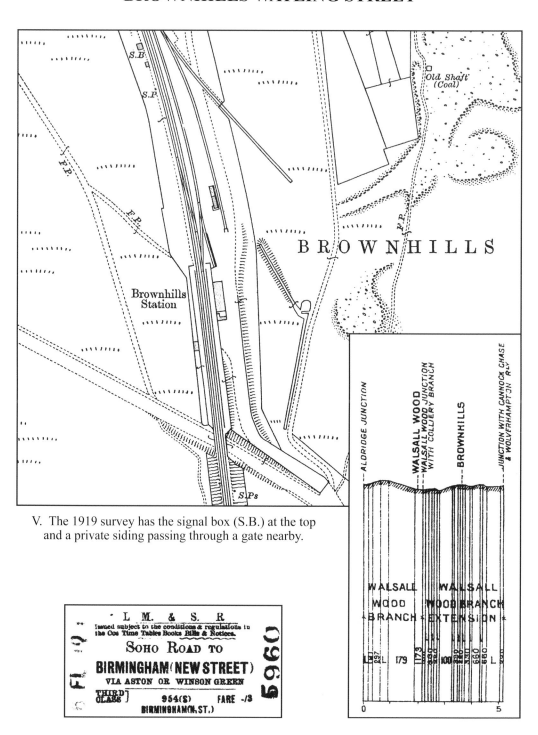

V. The 1919 survey has the signal box (S.B.) at the top and a private siding passing through a gate nearby.

6.   The station opened on 1st July 1884, but "Watling Street" was not added until 2nd June 1924. This was the name of the nearby Roman road from London to Holyhead, which became the A5 in 1919. In the distance is the goods yard, which closed on 31st March 1930, the same day that passenger service ceased on the branch. (N.Williams coll.)

7.   There were still four collieries linked to the branch in 1938, but decline followed. This is the view south in 1959 and the site was later totally cleared. (R.M.Casserley)

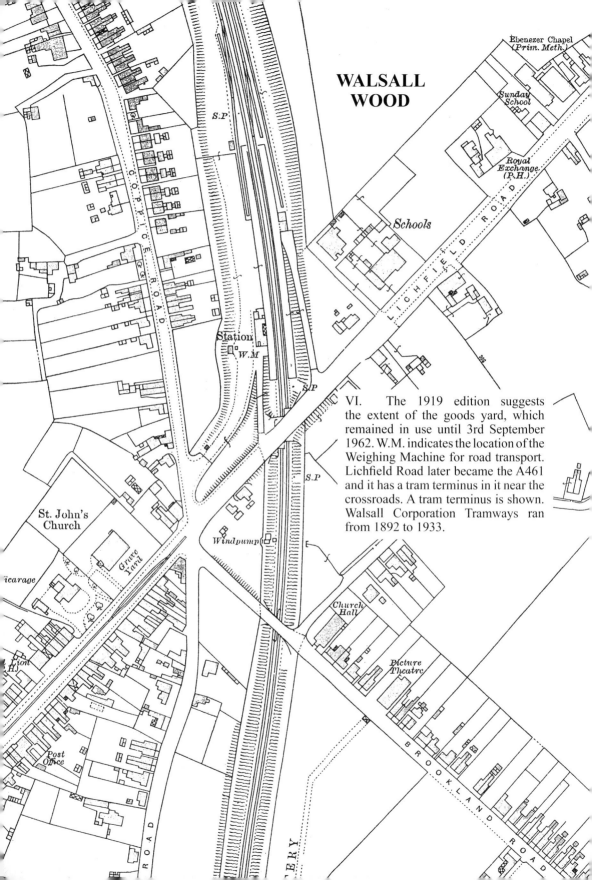

WALSALL WOOD

Ebenezer Chapel
(Prim. Meth.)

Sunday
School

Royal
Exchange.
(P.H.)

LICHFIELD ROAD

Schools

S.P

COPPICE ROAD

Station
W.M

S.P

S.P

St. John's
Church

Grave Yard

Windpump

icarage

Church
Hall

Picture
Theatre

Lion
H.)

Post
Office

BROOKLAND ROAD

ROAD

ERY

VI.   The 1919 edition suggests
the extent of the goods yard, which
remained in use until 3rd September
1962. W.M. indicates the location of the
Weighing Machine for road transport.
Lichfield Road later became the A461
and it has a tram terminus in it near the
crossroads. A tram terminus is shown.
Walsall Corporation Tramways ran
from 1892 to 1933.

8.   The 1874 Walsall Wood Colliery was served by both the MR via the Walsall Wood Branch and by the LNWR via a branch line to Norton Junction at Pelsall. The latter was closed when the colliery ceased working in October 1964. The picture shows a general view of the colliery from the southern approach. The Walsall Wood Branch continued to Brownhills Watling Street to the left of the picture which is from 1951. (CCHMS)

9.   This view south was taken from a special on 30th May 1959. Closure to passengers came on 31st March 1930 and to goods on 3rd September 1962. The station saw further use as a builder's store for Messrs. Southgate Engineering Ltd until demolition in the 1980s. Subsequently, the overbridge was in-filled and the area landscaped as children's playround. (G.Douglas)

10.   This September 1957 panorama is looking north with the colliery in the background. The Fowler 0-6-0 is working to Aldridge Junction with a loaded coal train. Singling took place in 1940. (P.Shoesmith)

ALDRIDGE

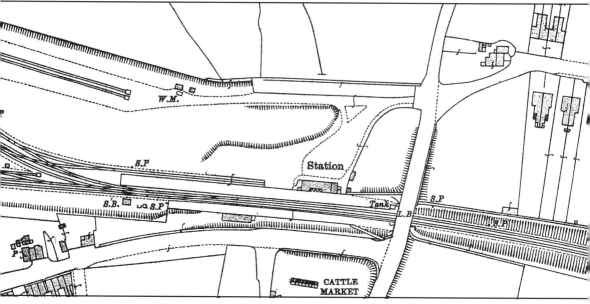

VII.   The 1914 edition has the main line from Wolverhampton runnning straight on the left, with the branch to Brownhills curving north.

11.   A postcard from LMS days has the goods yard on the left and the roofless facilities for gentlemen on the right. The crane was limited to lifting 30cwt. (P.Laming coll.)

12. This view from 26th May 1951 includes a railtour stopping for photography. The population rose from 2478 in 1901 to 56,850 in 1961. Private sidings numbered four to brickworks and two to wharves in 1938. They were north of Aldridge. (H.C.Casserley)

13. A train runs in behind 2-6-4T no. 42327. Near the bridge is the water tank, which was of particular value to locomotives working the branch. (W.A.Camwell/SLS coll.)

14. We are at Aldridge Junction, looking from the signal box towards Walsall on 25th May 1969. The Walsall Wood Branch curves away to the right past the ex-MR goods shed. The goods yard was closed to traffic on 7th December 1964. The branch was officially closed on 2nd August 1965, but the line was retained as far as the BICC sidings as an extended siding. It was used by BICC in conjunction with electrification works being carried out in the West Midlands before eventual closure on 15th November 1967, although various sources give the "official date" as 9th February 1969, when the last private siding closed. (D.Bathurst)

STREETLY

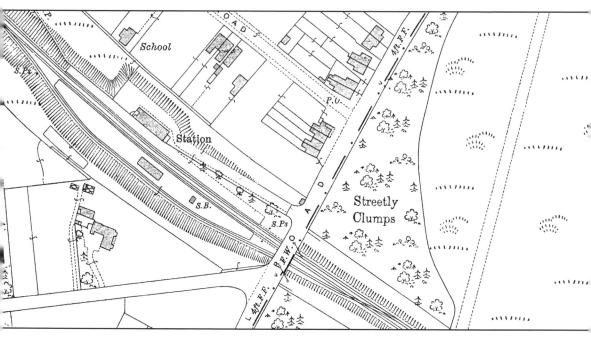

VIII. The 1914 edition shows that there was no access to the island platform from the road.

15.   We are looking towards Aldridge in 1908 with Hardwick Road Bridge in the distance. The newly laid track to the new island platform is visible. The station opened on 1st July 1879 and closed with the last train running on Saturday 16th January 1965 between Birmingham New Street and Walsall. By the early 1950s the island loop had been lifted and the signal box abolished. (A.Neath/Warwickshire Railways)

16.	Suggs Windsor pattern lamps add to the scene. A postcard from about 1910 appears to include an 0-6-4T. Nothing now remains standing. (P.Laming coll.)

17.	This view is of the up platform and the ex-MR main station building, looking towards Sutton Park on 16th January 1965. In 1957 Streetly, together with a temporary platform in the park, and Sutton Coldfield stations saw extensive use due to the World Jubilee Jamboree of the Boy Scout Movement to celebrate its 50th Anniversary, which was held in Sutton Park. For the duration of the event temporary block posts were set up at Streetly and Penns. (D.Bathurst)

SUTTON PARK

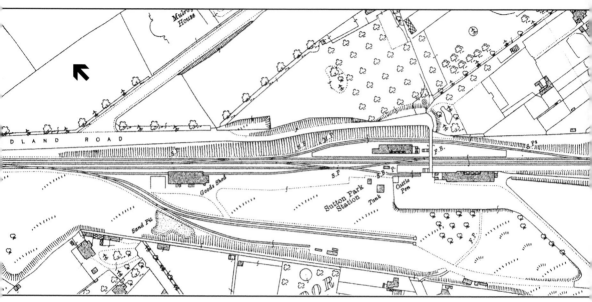

IX.   The park was given to the town by Bishop Kesey in 1528 and the proposal to bisect it with a railway met with fierce opposition. The benefits were eventually seen, notably cheaper coal. The joys of the park were available to Walsall folk on Sunday afternoons in 1944-64 with a shuttle service of up to six trains for part of the Summer. This is the 1913 edition at about 15ins to 1 mile.

18.   The station had an island platform on the up side. In this picture, we are looking towards Streetly, in the late 1940s with the ex-MR signal box and goods shed in the distance. No. 42448 waits with a Walsall to Birmingham local. The parcels traffic commenced with the station becoming a wartime distribution centre for the US Army. This was followed by a period acting in a similar capacity for the British services, before becoming a Post Office distribution centre in the 1950s. It continued in use as a PO depot until 1987, although general goods facilities were withdrawn on 7th December 1964. The station, however, continued to be used as offices well into the 1990s and was demolished in about 1999. (Warwickshire Railway coll.)

19. A panorama from the footbridge on 30th May 1959 includes the signal box, which was in use until 10th August 1969. Also featured is the massive distribution depot. (Milepost 92½)

20. Sadly we have no details of this parcels train running near the disused goods shed. The closed station is on the left and the forest of Sutton Park is encroaching on railway property, despite it having 2400 acres of land. (J.Whitehouse)

21. This 1980s photograph shows the straight double track making its way through Sutton Park, and the continued use of the goods shed and yard for parcels traffic. The goods yard was situated on the south side of the line to the west of the station. It included a brick-built goods shed, a cattle pen and a goods office. The parcel traffic was all by road after 1991 and much of it was then international. (S.Jones)

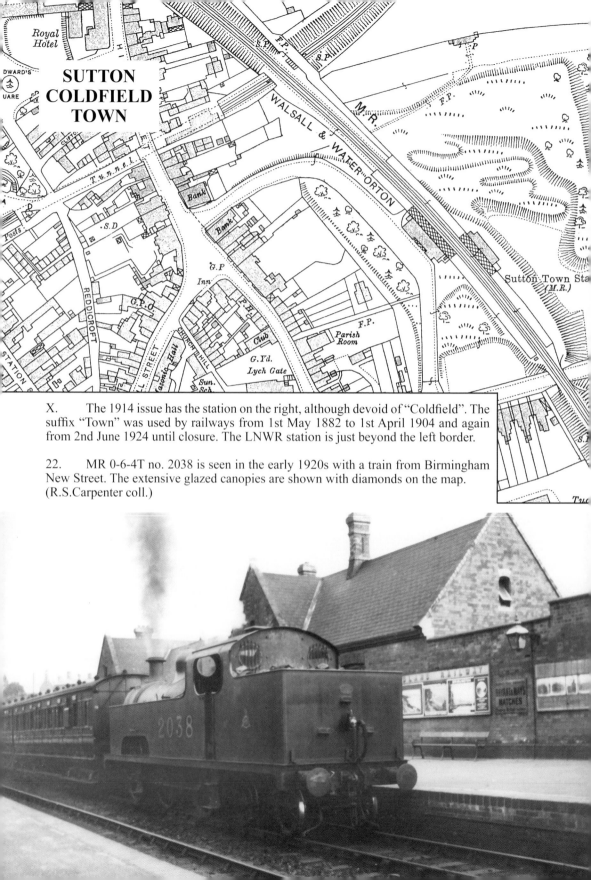

SUTTON
COLDFIELD
TOWN

Royal Hotel

Sutton Town Sta (M.R.)

X.   The 1914 issue has the station on the right, although devoid of "Coldfield". The suffix "Town" was used by railways from 1st May 1882 to 1st April 1904 and again from 2nd June 1924 until closure. The LNWR station is just beyond the left border.

22.   MR 0-6-4T no. 2038 is seen in the early 1920s with a train from Birmingham New Street. The extensive glazed canopies are shown with diamonds on the map. (R.S.Carpenter coll.)

23.　　The frontage was recorded in the 1950s. The station closed on 1st January 1925, however it saw use as a temporary measure as a result of the disaster which befell the diverted York-Bristol express at Sutton Coldfield station on Sunday 23rd January 1955. Passenger services ran for approximately a week after the accident. Kibby was a ladies' hairdressing salon. (J.Alsop)

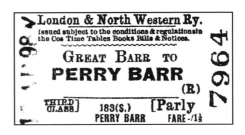

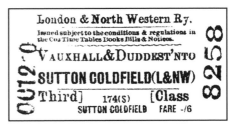

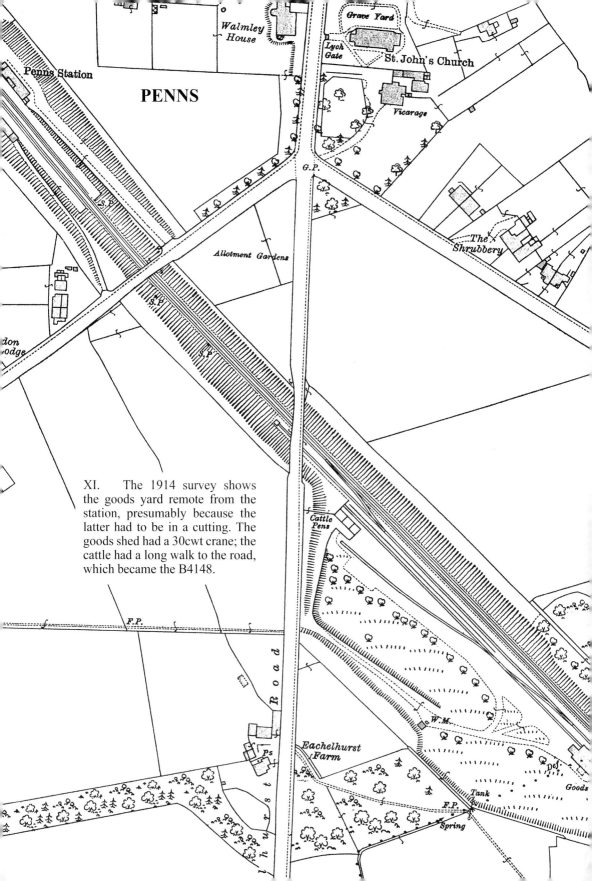

Penns Station

PENNS

Walmley House

Grave Yard

Lych Gate

St. John's Church

Vicarage

G.P.

Allotment Gardens

The Shrubbery

S.P.

S.P.

S.P.

don odge

XI. The 1914 survey shows the goods yard remote from the station, presumably because the latter had to be in a cutting. The goods shed had a 30cwt crane; the cattle had a long walk to the road, which became the B4148.

Cattle Pens

F.P.

Road

W.M.

Eachelhurst Farm

Ps

Goods

Def.

Tank

F.P.

Spring

24.   Standard MR architecture was employed, but their well known inclined fencing panels had not yet been introduced. The district is now urbanised, houses covering most of the map. (P.Laming coll.)

25.   Ambling through on 9th September 1954 is no. 43017, a class 4F 2-6-0 of a type introduced by the LMS in 1947. All the buildings were subsequently demolished. (Colour-Rail.com)

26.   A 2-car Glouces-
ter DMU passes Penns
goods shed with the
1.46pm Walsall to Bir-
mingham New Street
service on 2nd October
1959. The goods yard
closed on 1st February
1965. The goods shed
once contained a 30cwt
crane. The new white
building was used as a
store for cattle feed traffic for Messrs. R.Silcock.
Note the destination blind
is showing "Walsall"
and the 'B7' headcode
which was usually used
for services on the South
Staffs line. (M.Mensing)

27.   A Walsall bound DMU is seen on 16th January 1965, the last day of passenger services
between Birmingham New Street and Walsall via "The Park" line. Penns station was renamed "Penns
for Walmley" on 17th October 1936, but the suffix was discontinued in 1955. (D.Bathhurst)

28.   Park Lane Junction and the signal box were at the northeast corner of the triangular junction. The lines to Water Orton carry straight on, while those to Castle Bromwich can be seen curving away to the right. Both lines were singled in 1967. The signal box was abolished on 10th August 1969, the junction thereafter being controlled from the new Saltley Power Signal Box, itself now consigned to history. (B.Wright)

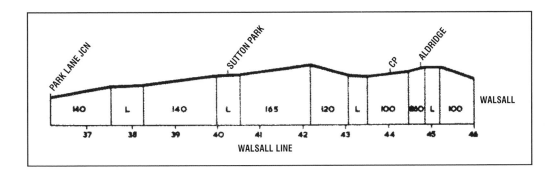

WATER ORTON

29.   The station opened much earlier than those seen so far, on 10th February 1842. The buildings presented here came into being in 1909, the earlier ones being nearer the junction. (P.Laming coll.)

XII. The 1918 edition is scaled at 15 inches to 1 mile and includes the trackbed of a line that once served a sewage works..

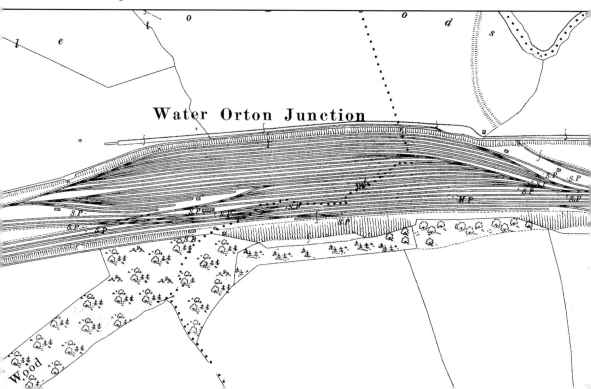

30.   These signals replaced those seen in the previous photograph. The signal box was superseded by the one seen on the back cover and in picture no. 32. (R.M.Casserley)

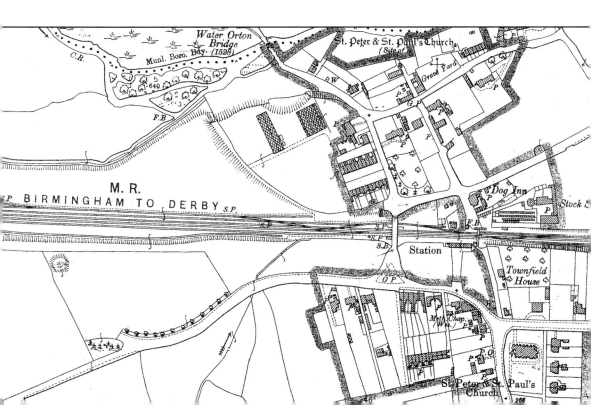

31. To the west of the station, the MR constructed extensive sidings. These were often used as a staging post for traffic using the Water Orton to Wolverhampton line. In this picture ex LMS class 4F 0-6-0 no. 44270 passes on a class F express freight on 16th August 1954. Water Orton yards closed between May and October 1968. (M.Norton)

32. The signal box was in use from 18th April 1943 until 10th August 1969. Passing it on 3rd May 1966 is class 8F 2-8-0 no. 48674. 624 of these locomotives were built from 1935 onwards. (R.Sivitier/ Colour-Rail.com)

33. A class 120 DMU calls on 16th April 1975 and is signalled to turn right to Walsall. In 2013, there were just five Leicester to Birmingham trains stopping at this platform, weekdays only, but more speeding straight on. The platforms can take five cars each. (A.Price/ Colour-Rail.com)

2. Bescot to Witton

PASSENGER SERVICES

Timetable extracts are shown to illustrate service evolution.

March 1850

September 1876

September 1925

August 1898

WOLVERHAMPTON, WALSALL, and BIRMINGHAM.—London and North Western.

Up	mrn	mrn	mrn	mrn	mrn	mrn	mrn	mrn	mrn	mrn	mrn	mrn	mrn	mrn	mrn	mrn	mrn	mrn	aft	aft	aft	aft	aft
	Tues., Thurs., and Saturdays.	Via Monument Lane.			Via Monument Lane.		Via Monument Lane.		Mondays only.	Via Monument Lane.			Via Monument Lane.		Via Monument Lane.	Manchester Express.			Via Monument Lane.	Except Saturdays.	Saturdays only.		Except Saturdays. Via Monument Lane.
High Level, Wolverhampton ..dep.						7 45			8 52		8 55			1015		1055	1110		1220			1 5	
Willenhall .....[Bridge						7 52					9 3			1022			a		1228			1 13	
Darlaston and James						7 56					9 7			1026			a		1232			1 16	
Wood Green						7 59					9 10			1029			a		1235			1 19	
Bescot ....arr.						8 2					9 13			1032			1130		1237			1 22	
Walsall 336, 334 arr.						8 15					9 58			1051			1145		1252			1 48	
Walsall 336, 334 dep.	6 10		7 0			8 5		8 30			9 18	9 45		1035	1040		1120	1135	1240			1 25	
Bescot ....dep.			7 4			8 9		8 35			9 23	9 51		1040	1045		1135	1140	1245			1 30	
Newton Road........			7 9			8 13		8 39			9 27				1049			1144				1 34	
Great Barr...........			7 14			8 17		8 43			9 31				1053		a	1148				1 38	
Perry Barr..........		6 44			8 2		8 36			9 12			9 53										1 56
Handsworth Wood..		6 48			8 8		8 40			9 15			9 57		1059				1255				2 2
Soho Road 333......		6 52			8 12		8 44			9 19			10 1		11 2				1258				2 6
Soho Road..........																				1256	1 21		
Handsworth Wood..																				1258	1 23		
Perry Barr ...[Grounds			7 18			8 21		8 47			9 35	10 0					a	1152		1 1	1 26	1 42	
Witton, fr Aston Lower						8 24		8 51			9 38							1155		1 4	1 29	1 45	
Aston 338............	6 25		7 21	7 26		8 26		8 54			9 41						1149	1158		1 7	1 32	1 48	
Stechford * 331.arr.			7 28														1154						
Vauxhall & Duddeston	6 30			7 30		8 31		8 59			9 44	10 8						12 3		1 11	1 35	1 53	
Birminghm (N.St.) 319	6 35	7 5		7 35	8 25	8 35	8 55	9 5	9 20	9 30	9 50	1013	1015	1057	1112	1120		12 8	1 8	1 15	1 40	2 0	2 18
319 London (Eus)..arr.			1010			1110					1235	2 20					2 45					4 40	

Up—Continued.	aft	aft	aft	aft	aft	aft	aft	aft	aft	aft	aft	aft	aft	aft	aft	aft	aft	aft	Sundays. mrn	mrn	aft	aft	aft	aft
	Saturdays only.		Via Monument Lane.		Via Monument Lane.		Via Monument Lane.		Via Monument Lane.															
High Level, Wolverhampton .dep.				2 57		4 15	4 55				6 25				8 45									
Willenhall ....[Bridge				3 5		4 22	5 1				6 32				8 53									
Darlaston and James				3 9		4 25	5 5				6 36				8 57									
Wood Green..........				3 12		4 28	5 8				6 39				9 0									
Bescot.... ....arr.				3 14		4 30	5 10				6 41				9 2									
Walsall 336, 334 arr.				3 53		4 58	5 47				7 0				9 17									
Walsall 336, 334 dep.		2 30		3 15	3 35	4 30	5 0	5 35	6 15		6 25		810		9 10		1035		9 50	1155	3 25	5 10	8 40	9 30
Bescot.............dep.		2 35		3 20	3 41	4 35	5 12	5 40			6 43		815		9 15		1040		9 55	12 0	3 30	5 15	8 45	
Newton Road.........		2 38			3 45	4 39		5 45					820		9 20		1044		9 59	12 5	3 35	5 20	8 49	
Great Barr		2 42			3 49	4 43		5 49			6 49		824		9 24		1048		10 4	1210	3 40	5 25	8 54	9 37
Perry Barr			2 58																					
Handsworth Wood..			3 2		3 56		5 21		6 29															
Soho Road 333.....			3 6		3 59		5 24		6 32															
Soho Road.........	2 1									642		741		846		9 57		1110						
Handsworth Wood..	2 3									645		745		848		10 0		1112						
Perry Barr...[Grounds	2 6	2 46		3 29		4 47		5 54		648	6 54	748	828	851	9 28	10 5	1052	1116	10 9	1215	3 45	5 30	8 59	9 41
Witton, fr Aston Lower	2 9	2 49						5 58		651		752	831											
Aston 338...	2 12	2 54				4 52		6 1		654	7 0	756	835	856	9 33	1010	1056	1120	1015	1220	3 50	5 34	9 4	9 45
Stechford *331 arr.											7 5													
Vauxhall & Duddeston	2 17	3 0				4 57		6 6		7 3		8 0	840	9 0	9 39	1016	11 1	1124	1020	1225	3 55	5 39	9 9	9 50
Birminghm (N.S.) 321	2 23	3 5	3 20	3 39	4 11	5 2	5 35	6 10	6 43	7 8		8 5	845	9 5	9 45	1020	11 5	1130	1025	1230	4 0	5 45	9 15	9 55
321 London (Eus.)...ar				6 35			8 30				9 45							3 50		4 35		9 0		3 50

a Stops to take up for South of Rugby on notice being given at the Station. * Station for Yardley.

September 1925

WOLVERHAMPTON, WALSALL, BESCOT, MONUMENT LANE, and BIRMINGHAM.—L. M. & S.

Miles	Up. Week Days.	mrn	mrn (Arrives Stechford at 7 29 mrn.)	mrn	mrn	mrn	mrn	mrn	mrn	mrn	mrn		aft	aft	aft	aft	aft T	aft	aft	aft	aft E	aft
	Wolverhampton......dep					7 32		8 10	8 52		1018				1227	1 10						
3	Willenhall (Bilston Street)					7 39		8 17	8 59		1026				1234	1 17			2 40			
4¾	Darlaston					7 43		8 21	9 4		1030				1238	1 21			2 43			
5¾	Wood Green					7 46		8 24	9 7		1033				1240	1 24			2 46			
6¾	Bescot ....arr.					7 50		8 28	9 11		1037				1245	1 28			2 50			
—	Walsall...............dep.	5 50	6 54	6 54	7 40	7 56	8 13	8 35	9 23	1028	1044		12 3	1210	1252	1 35	2 9	2 15	3 0	3 37	4 11	4 25
—	Bescot ....dep.	5 53	6 57	6 57		8 0		8 39	9 26		1048			1213	1256	1 39		2 18	3 3	3 41		4 29
7¾	Newton Road					8 4		8 43	9 30		1052			1217	1 0	1 44			3 7	3 45		4 33
9¾	Great Barr A	5 59	7 5	7 5		8 8	8 22	8 47	9 34		1056			1221	1 4	1 48			3 11	3 49		4 37
—	Mls. Handsworth Wood				7 52		8 26								1 9			2 27		3 54		
—	¾ Soho Road				7 56		8 30								1 13			2 31		3 57		
—	2 Winson Green				8 0		8 34								1 17					4 1		
—	2¾ Monument Lane				8 3		8 39								1 20			2 40		4 5		
11¼	Perry Barr.......[Grounds	6 3	7 9	7 9		8 12		8 51	9 38		11 0			1225		1 52			3 15			4 41
12¼	Witton, for Aston Lower	6 7	7 12	7 12		8 16		8 54	9 41					1228		1 55			3 18			
13	Aston 370	6 11	7 16	7 16		8 19		8 58	9 44		11 5			1231		1 59			3 21			4 48
14	Vauxhall and Duddeston	6 15		7 22		8 23		9 3	9 49		1110			1235		2 4			3 25			4 52
15½	Birmingham B 317 ..arr.	6 22		7 30	8 10	8 30	8 46	9 10	9 55	1050	1116		1220	1242	1 27	2 11	2 29	2 46	3 32	4 13	4 29	5 0
128	317 London (Euston)..arr.		10 0			1040			1240		1 25		3 a 0	3 a 0		4 35			6 35	6 50	6 50	

Up.	Week Days—Continued. aft	aft (Restaurant Car Express, Wolverhampton to London.)	aft	aft	aft		aft	aft	aft	aft				Sundays. mrn		aft	aft	aft	aft	
Wolverhampton..........dep.	4 35	5 40		5 58	6 21					10 5										
Willenhall (Bilston Street)	4 41			6 6	6 28					1012										
Darlaston	4 45			6 10	6 32					1015										
Wood Green	4 48			6 13	6 35					1018										
Bescot...............arr.	4 51	5 52		6 17	6 39					1022										
Walsall ....dep.	4 25	5b36	5 36	6 30	6 30		7 40	8 36	9 32	1034				9 53		1211	4 31	8 26	9 41	
Bescot...............dep.	4 52	5 54	5 40	6 33	6 41			8 39	9 35	1037				9 57		1215	4 34	8 30		
Newton Road	4 56		5 44					8 43		1041				10 1		1219	4 39	8 34		
Great Barr A	5 0		5 48	6 40	6 47			8 47	9 41	1045				10 5		1223	4 43	8 38	9 50	
Handsworth Wood	5 6			6 44			7 51													
Soho Road	5 11			6 48			7 54													
Winson Green	5 15			6 52			7 58													
Monument Lane	5 20			6 55			8 2													
Perry Barr ....[Grounds			5 52		6 52			8 51	9 45	1049				10 9		1228	4 47	8 43	9 54	
Witton, for Aston Lower			5 57					8 56												
Aston 370			6 1		7 0			9 0	9 51	1054				1015		1233	4 52	8 48	9 59	
Vauxhall and Duddeston			6 5		7 6			9 4	9 55	1058				1022		1238	4 57	8 53	10 3	
Birmingham 317 B ....arr.	5 28	6 11	6 14	7 2			8 10	9 11	10 3	11 6				1030		1246	5 5	9 2	1012	
317 London (Euston).....arr.		8 20	10 45				10e35			3d50				1 45		5 5	8 20		5 0	

A Station at Hamstead (2 miles from Great Barr).
a Arrives at 4 15 aft. on Saturdays.
B New Street; about ¼ mile to Moor Street and about ⅜ mile to Snow Hill Stations.
b Change at Bescot for Coventry and London.
d Arrives at 5 mrn. on Sundays.
E or *e* Except Saturdays.
S Saturdays only.
T Thursdays only.

BESCOT

34.   We are looking towards Great Barr in about 1961. Carriages were often to be seen berthed in the south bay platform - the "Up bay siding". The up yard was to the left of the picture while to the right were two down yards. There were no road-side buildings at Bescot, as the station was approached from two directions by footpaths, one of which crossed the River Tame from a nearby road. Like many of the "rivers" in the Black Country, its standard of cleanliness was once interesting to say the least! (I.Pell coll.)

35.   A view in the other direction on 4th September 1962 has the curve to Walsall in the distance and the steel lattice footbridge between the platforms. The gas lamps are Suggs Rochester pattern, which are shadowless. (B.W.L.Brooksbank)

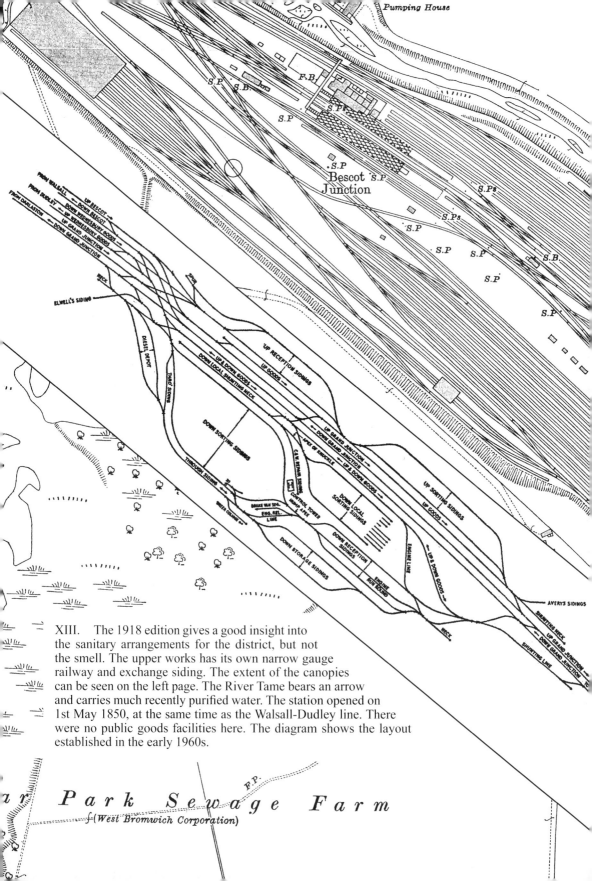

Pumping House

F.B.

S.P   S.B.

S.P

S.P

Bescot   S.P
Junction

S.Ps

S.Ps

S.P

S.P   S.P

S.P

S.B.

S.P

FROM WALSALL
FROM DUDLEY
FROM DARLASTON
UP BESCOT
DOWN BESCOT
UP WEDNESBURY GOODS
DOWN WEDNESBURY GOODS
UP GRAND JUNCTION
DOWN GRAND JUNCTION

ELWELL'S SIDING

DIESEL DEPOT

TMD SIDING

DOWN LOCAL SHUNTING NECK
UP & DOWN GOODS
UP RECEPTION SIDINGS
UP GOODS

DOWN SORTING SIDINGS

THROUGH SIDING

BRAKE VAN SDG.
ENG. REL.
LINE

C.W. REPAIR SIDINGS
APEX OF KNUCKLE
CONTROL TOWER
HUMP No.1

UP GRAND JUNCTION
DOWN GRAND JUNCTION
UP & DOWN GOODS

DOWN LOCAL
SORTING SIDINGS

UP SORTING SIDINGS
UP GOODS

DOWN STORAGE SIDINGS

DOWN RECEPTION
SIDINGS

ENGINE
RUN ROUND

ENGINE LINE

UP & DOWN GOODS

AVERYS SIDINGS

SHUNTING NECK
UP GRAND JUNCTION
DOWN GRAND JUNCTION
SHUNTING LINE

NECK

XIII.   The 1918 edition gives a good insight into
the sanitary arrangements for the district, but not
the smell. The upper works has its own narrow gauge
railway and exchange siding. The extent of the canopies
can be seen on the left page. The River Tame bears an arrow
and carries much recently purified water. The station opened on
1st May 1850, at the same time as the Walsall-Dudley line. There
were no public goods facilities here. The diagram shows the layout
established in the early 1960s.

Park Sewage Farm
(West Bromwich Corporation)

FP.

Munl. Boro. Bdy.

Co. & Parly. Boro. Bdy.

TRAMWAY

(Walsall Corporation)

Sewage

Farm

Filter

Filter

Sand Pit

Def.

Catchpits

14   1·713

F.P.

F.P.

S.P.

S.P.

S.P.

S.P.

S.P.

S.B.

S.P.

S.P.

S.P.

Sluice

Sluice

Slu.

S.P.

S.Ps.

S.P.

S.B.

36.   All the buildings were swept away along with the footbridge, prior to electrification. Electric trains began running to Walsall on 6th March 1967. No. 47344 is working a Merry-go-round coal train near the new building on 13th April 1978. (T.Heavyside)

Bescot Stadium

37.   The platforms were rebuilt for just four coaches each and yet more new buildings are evident on 26th June 2008. The suffix had been added on 16th August 1990, when the structures were completed for the new football facilities. There was a basic service of four trains each hour on weekdays, with two on Sundays. (V.Mitchell)

Freight yard

38.   The marshalling yard opened in 1892. We look from the footbridge over the Walsall to Bescot curve on 17th March 1962, as class 8F 2-8-0 no. 48733 comes off the Walsall line with a southbound freight. On the right, no. 48766 is heading towards the shed. Today, a slightly higher elevation could be obtained from the M6. (M.Mensing/I.Pell coll.)

39.   Ex-MR class 2P 4-4-0 no. 40646 sits in front of a stored locomotive adjacent to the "coal hole" at Bescot shed. The locomotive came to Bescot in 1960 and was allocated to Walsall Engineer's duties. As such it was kept in good condition. In 1961 no. 40646 gained a coal-railed tender. It was withdrawn in May 1962. In the background, beyond the Down yard, can be seen Bescot No. 5 signal box, itself closed when the yards were re-modelled on 5th December 1965. The photograph is from May 1962. (I.Pell coll.)

40.	The station footbridge is above us and the M6 is in the background, as no. 20004 runs in with mixed freight from the Walsall route in October 1976. The original GJR route is on the left. (J.Whitehouse)

41.	The upgrade of the yard was started in 1961 and completed in 1965. It included humps with 4300 automatic retarders, but these were only suitable for four-wheeled wagons. These were phased out and thus the system was not used after 1984. The yards had a capacity of 4000 wagons in 24 hours. The old reception sidings and the up secondary sorting sidings were converted to a virtual quarry for ballast. No. 25124 is departing on 13th April 1978. (T.Heavyside)

42.   No. 66091 is about to pass under the M6 on 21st July 2010 with a train from Wolverhampton Steel Terminal. It has just reversed on the "up and down goods loop", and is bound for Immingham Docks. (A.C.Hartless)

Steam Depot

43.   The shed had eight roads and initially, could accommodate 32 locomotives. By 1912, there was an allocation of 63, this increasing to 81 by 1923. In the background of this picture from 9th May 1936 is the then new coaling plant, which had a capacity of 75 tons. Central is ex-LNWR 4-6-2T no. 6957, which lasted until December 1957. (H.C.Casserley)

44.   Former 15-ton London Tilbury & Southend Railway crane (Works No. 2933) was allocated to Bescot from 1931. It was replaced on 1st May 1964 by crane No. RS 1075/30. Mock-up electrification sections, complete with non-powered cables were constructed at the depot to remind train crews about the limited clearances and are seen here to good advantage. (I.Pell coll.)

45.   This is a general view of the chaos that was Bescot MPD, especially on a Sunday afternoon. Bescot was mainly a freight engine depot serving the numerous freight workings from the associated yards. Until 1957, it did passenger turns on local workings, but on the dieselisation of these duties, its passenger workings were reduced to Saturday only or diesel substitutions. The mechanical coaling plant and the associated ash disposal plant continued in use until closure of the steam depot. (I.Pell coll.)

46.   A closer look at the coaling plant includes the ash handling equipment on the left. It facilitated the loading of the debris into wagons. Featured on 15th September 1963 is class G2a 0-8-0 no. 49361, complete with its tender cab for reverse running. (Colour-Rail.com)

47.   Class 2F 2-6-0 no. 46490 is seen in the foreground undertaking track work in conjunction with the re-development of the access to the down yards from the Wolverhampton, Walsall and Bescot curve lines. The picture also illustrates the 1960s replacement crane in use on 26th August 1964. The shed closed to steam on 28th March 1966. Part of the 42ft turntable is evident. (B.Matthews)

Diesel Depot

48.	The steam shed is seen in February 2004, long after it had been fenced off. Demolition commenced in November 2013. (Colour-Rail.com)

49.	A lazy Sunday afternoon at the TMD is seen in about 1977, with a large number of class 08 shunters and a single class 47. At this time, it was not unusual for main line locomotives to be stabled in the Holding Sidings, which at this time were located in the DLSS (Down Local Storage Sidings). The yard shunters and those used at local yards, tended to run at weekends to the depot, hence the large number visible. (I.Pell)

50. No. 31203 stands by the TMD on 3rd March 1996, its left cab being at the end of the refuelling bay. Transrail was a BR freight subsidiary. (M.Turvey)

51. EWS is English Welsh and Scottish Railways and its no. 66074 passes the new diesel depot on 27th March 1999. Beyond the left border of this view was Bescot Down Tower, which controlled movements to and from the yards from 6th December 1965 until 24th September 2013. (M.Turvey)

52. By 21st July 2010, the diesel depot was quiet and lifeless. (A.C.Hartless)

TAME BRIDGE PARKWAY

53.   The station opened on 4th June 1990, but the suffix was not added until 1st June 1997. Bescot Yards commence just beyond the A4031 bridge in this northward view from 26th August 2008. The platforms were built for five coaches, insufficient for W&SR trains in 2008-11. This train will run non-stop to Wolverhampton, having bypassed Birmingham. They called at 12.38, 14.38, 18.38 and 22.14. (V.Mitchell)

54.   Running through towards Bescot on 5th May 2012 are nos 20312 and 20308 with the "Hampshire Hopscotch" tour. It ran from Crewe to the docks at Southampton, via Banbury. The bridge carries the Tame Valley Canal aqueduct. (J.Whitehouse)

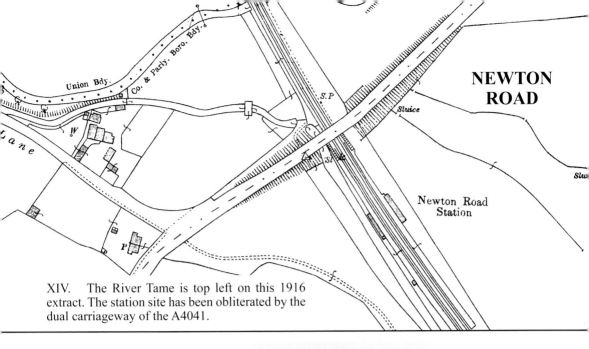

NEWTON ROAD

XIV. The River Tame is top left on this 1916 extract. The station site has been obliterated by the dual carriageway of the A4041.

55. We are looking towards Great Barr on 5th August 1930. A station opened here on 4th July 1837, but no sidings were provided. A new one was brought into use on 1st March 1863, a little to the north. The one seen functioned from 1st January 1902 until 7th May 1945. (R.S.Carpenter coll.)

56. This crossing was south of the station and the box was in use until 6th December 1965. The multitude of insulators on the cross bars were due to the lack of insulated wires. (H.Hazlewood/N.Williams coll.)

HAMSTEAD

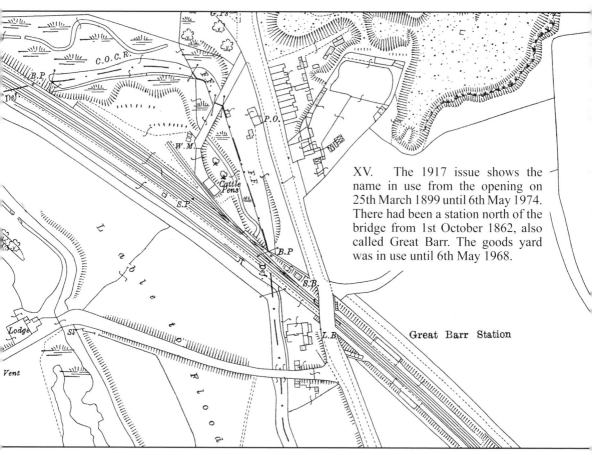

XV.   The 1917 issue shows the name in use from the opening on 25th March 1899 until 6th May 1974. There had been a station north of the bridge from 1st October 1862, also called Great Barr. The goods yard was in use until 6th May 1968.

Great Barr Station

57.   This view of the staff is from the south and it includes the steps to the up platform. The others are evident on the map. The signal box is also included. (P.Laming coll.)

58.　Captured in the 1960s is this grimy class 2F 2-6-0 numbered 46427. It was working from Birmingham New Street to Walsall. The box was in use until 4th July 1966. The new and higher bridge is under construction. It is on the western boundary of the City of Birmingham. (W.A.Camwell/SLS coll.)

59.　Prior to electrification, the canopy width was reduced and a footbridge (left) was built. EMU no. 323204 is working the 14.31 Birmingham New Street to Walsall service on 14th June 2010. The up platform takes six cars and the down one five. (A.C.Hartless)

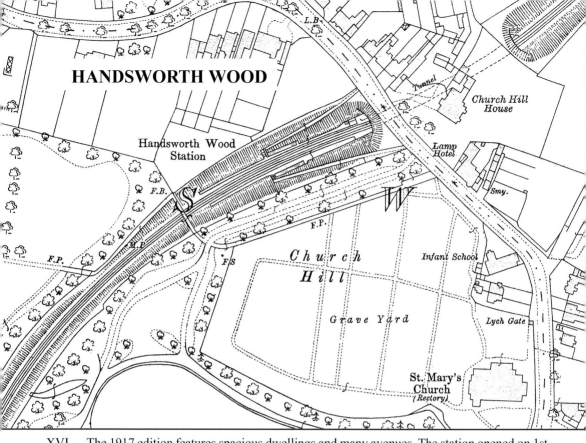

HANDSWORTH WOOD

Handsworth Wood
Station

Church Hill House

Lamp Hotel

Tunnel

Smy.

Church
Hill

Infant School

Grave Yard

Lych Gate

St. Mary's
Church
(Rectory)

L.B.

F.B.

F.P.

F.P.

M.P.

F.S.

XVI.   The 1917 edition features spacious dwellings and many avenues. The station opened on 1st January 1896 and closed on 5th May 1941 as a wartime economy measure, but it never reopened.

60.   The map shows that the bridge carries a public footpath and it also shows the two long paths to the platforms. We can enjoy the rural scene and the peaceful graveyard. (P.Laming coll.)

61.   The panorama from the footbridge includes a crowd leaving a Birmingham-bound train. At times the staff must have been busy with their scythes. (P.Laming coll.)

SOHO ROAD

XVII.   We turn south at the triangular junction to visit the Soho and Perry Barr line. The southern station is seen on the 1917 edition, as is the connection curving sharply to the Soho Pool Wharf.

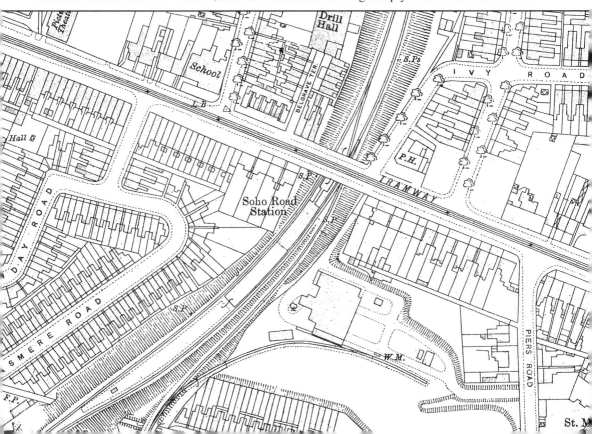

62.   This is a northward view from 28th June 1929 and it has the goods line to Soho Pool on the right. Its starting signal is to the right of the canopy. (R.A.Carpenter coll.)

SOHO POOL

63.   No. D8134 stands with the REC brake van special on 27th April 1968. This extensive goods yard was accessed via a single track branch line from Soho Road Junction. The terminus had timber, coal yards and a Regent Oil terminal. The yard was closed to general freight from 6th May 1974 and oil traffic ceased on 7th July 1982, when the branch was taken out of use. Soho Pool Wharf, as it was originally known opened on 1st April 1889. (D.Bathurst)

PERRY BARR

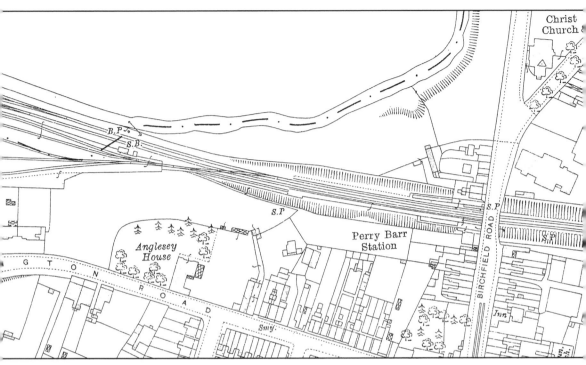

XVIII. We return to the 1837 main line. Birchfield Road bridge has been widened to take a dual carriageway and a massive roundabout is now lower right, serving the A34 and A4040. This is another 1917 extract and it includes the River Tame.

64.   This was the peaceful road in Edwardian days, with only horse droppings to be a nuisance. The station opened on 4th July 1837 and had access from the bridge from the outset. (P.Laming coll.)

65.   The station opened with the line and is still in use. Its up platform takes seven coaches and its down one five. The eastward view is probably from the 1920s. The station was modernised in the early 1960s, when the houses were demolished at the time of road widening. (P.Laming coll.)

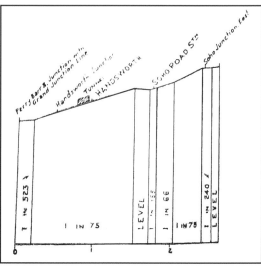

66.   "Patriot" class 4-6-0 no. 45546 *Fleetwood* is running east, sometime in the 1950s. In the background is part of the goods yard, which closed around 1960. Also evident is Perry Bar Station Junction Box, which was in use until 4th July 1966. (W.A.Camwell/SLS coll.)

67. Featureless flat roofed buildings appeared at the time of electrification. (J.Whitehouse)

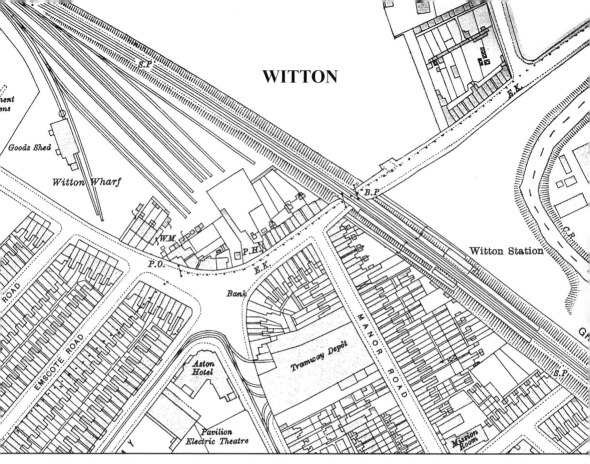

WITTON

Goods Shed

Witton Wharf

Witton Station

Aston Hotel

Tramway Depot

Pavilion Electric Theatre

Bank

XIX.   This 1917 extract includes details of the tram depot, but the signal box is beyond the top left corner. It was in use until 4th July 1966 and was called Witton Goods. The yard closed on 5th October 1970, but was coal only in its final five months. It had a 20-ton crane to serve the local heavy industry. It was later reopened for stone traffic from Caldon Low until February 1989.

68.   This view towards the goods yard is from 5th August 1930. The station had opened on 1st May 1876 and was to serve Aston Villa Football Club. Aston will be visited in pictures 81-86. (R.S.Carpenter coll.)

69.　　Nearby was one of the large works of Imperial Chemical Industries. Its Ramsbottom 0-4-0T no. 4 carries the firm's logo. (Milepost 92½)

70.　　Arriving at 14.01 on 24th August 2009 is no. 323215, while a freight train runs towards Aston. A football logo is near the words "Villa Park". (J.Whitehouse)

3. Birmingham to Lichfield

PASSENGER SERVICES

Eng., Henry Woodhouse.]   **SUTTON COLDFIELD BRANCH.**—London and North Western.

Fares. a 3rd class to Stafford,				Week Days.									Sundays.			RETURN TICKETS.—1st cl., 1s.6d ; 2nd, 1s.3d.; 3rd, 1s.2d. Down.										Sundays.		
1cl.	2cl.	3cl.	L'pool & Manchester.	1,2,3	1,2,3	1,2,3	1,2,3	1,2,3	1,2,3	1,2,3	1,2,3	1,2,3	1,2,3	1,2,3	1,2,3	New Street Station.	mrn	mrn	gov	aft	aft	aft	aft	aft		mrn	gov	aft
s.d.	s.d.	s.d.		mrn	a	mrn	b	gov	aft	aft	mrn	gov	mrn	gov		Birmingham	7 20	8 40	10 0	1 54	20	6 15	7 35	9 10		9 0	2 35	7 30
0 3	0 2	0 1	Sutton Coldfield	8 0	9 20	1045	2 20	5	0 5	5 50	8 15	9 45	9 50	6	0 8 15	Bloomsbury&Neckells	..	..	10 4	..	..	..	..	..		..	2 39	..
9	4 0	3 0	Wylde Green	8 4	9 24	1049	2 24	5	4 6	5 48	19 9	4	9 54	6	4 8 19	Aston	7 27	8 47	10 12	1 12	4	27	6 22	7 42	9 17		9 7	2 47	7 37
0 6	4 0	2 4	Chester Road	8 7	9 27	1052	2 27	5	7 6	5 7	8	22 9	5 3	9 57	6	7 8 22	Gravelly Hill	7 31	8 51	10 16	1 16	4	31	6 26	7 46	9 21		9 11	2 51	7 41
0 8	5 0	3 2	Erdington	8 11	9 31	1056	2 31	5	11 7	0 8	26	9 56	10	1	6 11 8 26	Erdington	7 34	8 54	10 19	1 19	4	34	6 29	7 49	9 24		9 14	2 54	7 44
0 10	7 0	5	Aston 139	8 18	9 38	11 3	2 38	5	18 7	7 8	33	10 4	10	8	6 18 8 33	Chester Road	7 38	8 58	10 23	1 23	4	38	6 33	7 53	9 28		9 18	2 58	7 48
1 0		9 0 6	Bloomsbry & Nechells	9 41	..	..	..	5	22	..	..	..	..	..	6 21 8 37	Wylde Green	7 42	9	2	10 27	1 27	4	42	6 37	7 57	9 32		9 22	3 2	7 52
1 0		9 6½	Lawley St. [115, 154]	144	..	..	..	5	26	..	..	..	..	..	6 25 ..	Sutton Coldfield	7 50	9	10	10 35	1 35	4	50	6 45	8	5 9	37		9 30	3 10	8 0
1 0		9 0 7	Birminghm 109,	8 30	9 50	1115	2 50	5	35 7	20	8	48	1020	1020	6 35 8 50														

WALSALL, SUTTON COLDFIELD, LICHFIELD, BURTON, and DERBY.—L. & N.W.

The November 1865 timetable shows the service before the route was extended to Lichfield.

September 1885.

BIRMINGHAM, SUTTON COLDFIELD, and LICHFIELD.—L. M. & S.

September 1925.

A Station for Oscott College (1¼ miles).	**b** Arrives at 5 36 aft.
a Arrives at 8 45 mrn.	**E** Except Saturdays.
	S Saturdays only.
	W Wednesdays and Saturdays.

BIRMINGHAM, SUTTON COLDFIELD, and LICHFIELD

Miles		Week Days																							Sundays									
		a.m	a.m	am	a.m	p.m	p.m E	p.m S	p.m W	p.m S	pm	p.m	pm S	pm E	pm E	pm	pm E	p.m	p.m E	p.m E	pm	p.m	pm	p.m D	a.m	a.m	p.m	pm B	pm B	p.m	pm B	p.m	pm B	p.m
—	**Birmingham** (New St.). dep	6 20	7 50	850	9 45	1210	1225	1243	1 15	1 20	215	4 12	418	448	515	526	540	6 0	6 33	6 45	723	8 36	845	10 0	9 25	1150	2 25	255	425	5 5	620	7 35	820	1050
1¼	Vauxhall and Duddeston...	6 23	7 53	854	9 48	1213	1228	1246	1 18	1 23	218	4 15	421	451	..	529	544	6 3	6 36	6 48	726	8 39	848	10 3	9 28	1153	2 28	258	428	5 8	623	7 38	823	..
2½	Aston	6 28	7 57	858	9 53	1217	1232	1250	1 22	1 27	222	4 19	425	455	..	533	549	6B11	6 40	6 52	730	8 43	852	10 7	9 32	1157	2 32	3 2	432	5 12	627	7 42	827	1057
4	Gravelly Hill..............	6 32	8 1	9 2		1221	1236	1254	1 26		226		429	459	..	537	554	6 15		6 56	734		856	1011		..	..	..	..	..	..		..	..
5	Erdington	6A41	8 7	9 6	Via Walsall (Tables 77 & 83)	1225	1240	1258	1 30	Via Walsall (Tables 77 & 83)	230	Via Walsall (Tables 77 & 83)	433	5 3	..	541	558	6 19	Via Walsall (Tables 77 & 83)	7 0	738	Via Walsall (Tables 77 & 83)	9 0	1015	Via Walsall (Tables 77 & 83)	12 7	2 40	310	440	5 20	635	Via Walsall (Tables 77 & 83)	835	11 5
5½	Chester Road A............	6 44	8 10	9 9		1228	1243	1 1	1 33		233		436	5 6	..	544	6 2	6 22		7 3	741		9 3	1018		1210	2 43	313	443	5 23	638		838	11 8
6½	Wylde Green..............	6 47	8 13	912		1231	1246	1 4	1 36		236		439	5 9	529	547	6 6	6 26		7 6	745		9 7	1022		1213	2 46	316	446	5 26	641		841	1111
7½	**Sutton Coldfield**..........	6 52	8 18	917		1236	1252	1 9	1 41		241		444	516	533	551	611	6 31		7 11	750		911	1027		1218	2 51	321	451	5 31	646		847	1117
8¾	Four Oaks..................	6 59	8 23	922		1241	1257	1 14	1 46		246		449	522	539	556	616	6 36		7 16	755		916	1033		1223	2 56	326	456	5 36	651		852	1122
10¾	Blake Street................	7 4	8 28	927		..	1 2	1 19	..		251		454	527	544	6 1	..	6 41		..	8 0		..	1038		..	..	..	..	..	..		..	..
13¼	Shenstone....................	7 9	8 33	932		..	1 7	1 24	..		256		459	532	551	6 6	..	6 46		..	8 5		..	1043		1233	3 6	..	..	..	..		..	..
16½	**Lichfield** (City)......... arr	7 16	8 40	939	1052	..	1 14	1 31	..	2 21	3 3	5 17	5 6	539	558	613	..	6 53	7 43	..	812	9 44	..	1050	1025	1240	3 13	..	..	..	..	8 49	..	..

Miles		Week Days																						Sundays								
		a.m E	a.m	am	a.m	a.m	a m	a.m	am	am	a.m	p.m S	pm	p.m	p.m	p.m S	p.m	p.m	p.m S	p.m	p.m E	p.m	p.m	p.m	p.m B	p.m	p.m B	p.m	p.m B	p.m B	p.m	
—	**Lichfield** (City)......... dep	..	6 23	655	..	7 25	7 41	8 0	..	9 9	11 4	1214	..	1 6	1 47	2 31	4 16	5 11	6 15	6 23	6 55	8 43	9 0	1 15	..	3 45	..	..	..	..	9 0	..
3	Shenstone....................	..	6 30	7 2	..	..	7 47	8 6	..	915	11 10	1220	..		1 53		4 23	5 17	..	6 29	7 2	8 49		1 21	..	3 51	..	..	..	..		..
5½	Blake Street.................	..	6 38	710	..		7 53	8 12	..	921	11 16	1226	..		1 59		4 29	5 23		6 35	..	8 55		..	..	..	..	..	..	..		..
7½	Four Oaks....................	6 10	6 46	717	7 45	Via Walsall (Tables 83 & 77)	7 59	8 18	828	927	11 22	1232	112	Via Walsall (Tables 83 & 77)	2 5	Via Walsall (Tables 83 & 77)	4 35	5 29	Via Walsall (Tables 83 & 77)	6 41	7 15	9 1	Via Walsall (Tables 83 & 77)	1 34	3 37	4 3	5 5	5 42	7 10	9 2	Via Walsall (Tables 83 & 77)	..
8½	**Sutton Coldfield**...........	6 13	6 51	721	7 49		8 3	8 22	831	931	11 26	1236	117		2 9		4 39	5 34		6 45	7 19	9 5		1 38	3 40	4 7	5 8	5 45	7 13	9 5		..
10	Wylde Green................	6 17	6 55	725	7 53		8 7	8 26	835	935	11 30	1240	121		2 13		4 43	5 38		6 49	7 23	9 9		1 42	3 44	4 11	5 12	5 49	7 17	9 9		..
10¾	Chester Road A............	6 20	6 58	728	7 56		8 10	..	838	938	11 33	1243	124		2 16		4 46	5 41		6 52	7 26	9 12		1 45	3 47	4 14	5 15	5 52	7 20	9 12		..
11¼	Erdington	6 23	7 1	731	7 59		8 13	..	841	941	11 36	1246	127		2 19		4 49	5 44		6 56	7 30	9 15		1 48	3 50	4 17	5 18	5 55	7 23	9 15		..
12½	Gravelly Hill...............	6 26	7 4	734	8 2		8 16	..	844	944	11 39	1249	130		2 22		4 52	5 47		6 59	..	9 18		..	..	..	..	..	..	..		..
13¾	Aston	6 30	7 8	738	8 6		8 20	..	848	950	11 43	1253	134	2 0	2 26	3 35	4 56	5 51		7 5	7 36	9 22	9:58	1 55	3 57	4 24	5 25	6 2	7 30	9 22	9 51	..
15	Vauxhall and Duddeston...	6 37	7 15	745	8B14	..	8 27	8B41	855	957	11B51	1 B 1	140	2 B 8	2 34	3H46	5 2	6A0	..	7 12	7 43	9J32	10B6	2 1	4B5	4 30	5B33	6B10	7H41	9B30	9 58	..
16½	**Birmingham** (New St.)..arr	6 42	7 20	750	8 19	8 19	8 36	8 46	9 0	102	11 56	1 6	146	2 13	2 39	3 51	5 7	6 6	7 19	7 17	7 48	9 37	1011	2 6	4 10	4 35	5 46	6 15	7 46	9 35	10 3	..

A Station for Oscott College (1¼ miles). A Arr. 5 minutes *earlier* **B** Commences 18th June B Arr. 4 minutes *earlier* **D** 30 minutes later on Sats. **E** or E Except Saturdays. H Arr. 7 minutes *earlier* J Arr. 6 minutes *earlier* **S** or S Saturdays only **W** Wednesdays and Saturdays only.

June 1950.

BIRMINGHAM TO SUTTON COLDFIELD AND LICHFIELD

Miles.		WEEKDAYS																	
				SX	SO	SX	SO				SO	SX					SO		
		a.m.	a.m.	a.m.	a.m.	a.m.	a.m. (T.V.—Birmingham to Lichfield)	a.m.	a.m.	a.m.	a.m.	a.m.	a.m.	a.m.	a.m.	a.m.	p.m.	p.m.	p.m.
0	**BIRMINGHAM New Street** ...dep.	6 22	6 52	7 19	7 22	7 43	7 52	8 22	8 52	9 22	9 52	9 58	10 22	10 58	11 22	11 52	12 5	12 22	12 52
1¼	Vauxhall and Duddeston ...... Z......	6 26	6 56	7 23	7 26	7 47	7 56	8 26	8 56	9 26	9 56	10 2	10 26	11 2	11 26	11 56	12 9	12 26	12 56
2½	Aston	6 29	6 59	7 26	7 29	7 50	7 59	8 29	8 59	9 29	9 59	10 5	10 29	11 5	11 29	11 59	12 12	12 29	12 59
4	Gravelly Hill	6 32	7 2	7 29	7 32	7 53	8 2	8 32	9 2	9 32	10 2	10 8	10 32	11 8	11 32	12 2	12 15	12 32	1 2
5	Erdington	6 36	7 6	7 33	7 36	7 57	8 6	8 36	9 6	9 36	10 6	10 12	10 36	11 12	11 36	12 6	12 19	12 36	1 6
5½	Chester Road	6 38	7 8	7 35	7 38	7 59	8 8	8 38	9 8	9 38	10 8	10 14	10 38	11 14	11 38	12 8	12 21	12 38	1 8
6¼	Wylde Green	6 40	7 10	7 37	7 40	8 1	8 10	8 40	9 10	9 40	10 10	10 16	10 40	11 16	11 40	12 10	12 23	12 40	1 10
7½	**Sutton Coldfield**	6 43	7 13	7 40	7 43	8 4	8 13	8 43	9 13	9 43	10 13	10 19	10 43	11 19	11 43	12 13	12 26	12 43	1 13
8¾	Four Oaks	6 47	7 17	7 44	7 47	8 8	8 17	8 47	9 17	9 47	10 17	10 23	10 47	11 23	11 47	12 17	12 30	12 47	1 17
10	Butlers Lane	6 50	...	7 47	7 50	8 11	8 20	8 50	9 20	9 50	...	...	10 50	...	11 50	...	12 33	12 50	1 20
10¾	Blake Street	6 52	.	7 49	7 52	8 13	8 22	8 52	9 22	9 52	.	.	10 52	.	11 52	.	12 35	12 52	1 22
13¼	Shenstone	6 57	...	7 54	7 57	8 18	8 27	8 57	9 27	9 57	...	...	10 57	...	11 57	...	12 40	12 57	1 27
16¼	**LICHFIELD City** .... arr.	7 3	7 27	8 0	8 3	8 24	8 33	9 5	9 33	10 3	.	.	11 3	.	12 3	.	12 46	1 3	1 33
17½	73LICHFIELD Trent Valley .... arr.	...	...	8 22	8 22	...	8 37	9 22	...	...	...	...	11S027	...	...	...	...	...	...

The extract from June 1964 indicates that a regular interval service began during the morning, but that trains terminated at Lichfield City. The connecting trains to Trent Valley had come from Wolverhampton via Walsall. There was an hourly service from 1.0pm on Sundays.

The CrossCity service from Redditch began in May 1978 and an afternoon sample is shown. There were two trains per hour, between Longbridge and Four Oaks only, on Sundays.

Redditch and Longbridge to Birmingham, Four Oaks and Lichfield

A Not Saturdays 13 May to 30 September
B Until 30 September
C From 7 October

			A	B SO			SX	SO				SO		SX	SX	SO		B SO	SX	C SO		SX	SX	B SO
Redditch	d	..	..	..	..	..	..	..	..	..	..	..	..	..	..	..	..	..	..	..	..	..	..	..
Alvechurch	d	..	..	..	..	..	..	..	..	..	..	..	..	..	..	..	..	..	..	..	..	..	..	..
Barnt Green	d	..	..	..	..	..	..	..	..	..	..	..	..	..	..	..	..	..	..	..	..	..	..	..
Longbridge	d	14 59	15 10	15 13	..	15 29	15 42	15 42	..	15 59	16 10	16 29	..	16 32	16 42	16 42	..	16 54	..	16 59	..	17 04	17 10	17 04
Northfield	d	15 02	15 13	15 16	..	15 32	15 45	15 45	..	16 02	16 13	16 32	..	16 35	16 45	16 45	..	16 57	..	17 02	..	17 07	17 13	17 07
King's Norton	d	15 05	15 16	15 20	..	15 35	15 48	15 48	..	16 05	16 16	16 35	..	16 38	16 48	16 48	..	17 00	..	17 05	..	17 10	17 16	17 10
Bournville	d	15 08	15 19	15 23	..	15 38	15 51	15 51	..	16 08	16 19	16 38	..	16 41	16 51	16 51	..	17 03	17 04	17 08	..	17 13	17 19	17 13
Selly Oak	d	15 11	15 22	15 26	..	15 41	15 54	15 54	..	16 11	16 22	16 41	..	16 44	16 54	16 54	..		17 07	17 11	..	17 16	17 22	17 16
University	d	15 14	15 25	15 28	..	15 44	15 57	15 57	..	16 14	16 25	16 44	..	16 47	16 57	16 57	..	17 07	17 09	17 14	..	17 19	17 25	17 19
Five Ways	d	15 18	15 29		..	15 48	16 01	16 01	..	16 18	16 29	16 58	..	16 51	17 01	17 01	..		17 13	17 18	..	17 23	17 29	17 23
Birmingham New Street	a	15 24	15 35	15 38	..	15 54	16 07	16 07	..	16 24	16 35	16 54	..	16 59	17 07	17 07	..	17 17	17 20	17 24	..	17 29	17 35	17 29
70	d	15 27	15 40	15 40	..	15 57	16 10	16 10	..	16 27	16 40	16 57	..	17 03	17 12	17 12	..	17 27	17 27	17 27	..	17 33	17 39	17 40
Duddeston 70	d	15 31			..	16 01	16 14	16 14	..	16 31	16 44	17 01	..	17 07	..	..	..	17 31	17 31	17 31	..	17 37	17 43	
Aston 70	d	15 34	15 45	15 45	..	16 04	16 17	16 17	..	16 34	16 47	17 04	..	17 10	17 18	17 17	..	17 34	17 34	17 34	..	17 41	17 46	17 45
Gravelly Hill	d	15 38	15 49	15 49	..	16 08	16 21	16 21	..	16 38	16 51	17 08	..	17 14	..	17 21	..	17 38	17 38	17 38	..	..	17 50	17 49
Erdington	d	15 41	15 52	15 52	..	16 11	16 24	16 24	..	16 41	16 54	17 11	..	17 17	..	17 24	..	17 41	17 41	17 41	..	17 47	17 53	17 52
Chester Road	d	15 44	15 55	15 55	..	16 14	16 27	16 27	..	16 44	16 57	17 14	..	17 20	17 26	17 27	..	17 44	17 44	17 44	..	17 49	17 56	17 55
Wylde Green	d	15 46	15 57	15 57	..	16 16	16 29	16 29	..	16 46	16 59	17 16	..	17 22	17 28	17 29	..	17 46	17 46	17 46	..	17 52	17 58	17 57
Sutton Coldfield	d	15 49	16 00	16 00	..	16 19	16 32	16 32	..	16 49	17 02	17 19	..	17 25	17 31	17 32	..	17 49	17 50	17 49	..	17 55	18 01	18 00
Four Oaks	d	15a33	16a03	16a03	..	16 22	16 35	16a35	..	16a53	17a05	17 22	..	17 29	17 35	17a35	..	17 52	17a53	17 52	..	17 59	18a04	18a03
Butlers Lane	d	..	..	..	..	16 26	16 39	..	..	..	..	17 26	..	..	17 39	..	..	17 56	..	17 56	..	18 03	..	..
Blake Street	d	..	..	..	..	16 28	16 41	..	..	..	..	17 28	..	..	17 41	..	..	17 58	..	17 58	..	18 05	..	..
Shenstone	d	..	..	..	..	16 32	16 45	..	..	..	..	17 32	..	..	17 46	..	..	18 02	..	18 02	..	18 10	..	..
Lichfield City	a	..	..	..	..	16 38	16 51	..	..	..	..	17 38	..	17 39	17 51	..	..	18 07	..	18 07	..	18 15	..	..

BIRMINGHAM NEW STREET

XX.   New Street and its station are lower left on this 1946 map at 6ins to 1 mile. Above them are the cathedral and Snow Hill station of the GWR. Its Moor Street station is to the right of New Street, the lines from which pass under the former and still do, but few passengers are aware of this. South of Curzon Street Goods Depot is Proof House junction, named after the gun certification premises, which has functioned for around 200 years. Our route to Aston curves above the eastbound lines. The square building north of Fazeley Street bridge is the original L&BR terminus, shown in picture 76. Trains bound for Aston climb onto the 1893 Lawley Street Viaduct to pass over the many goods lines. Top right is the LMS Windsor Street Goods Depot, which was served by a line from Aston until closure on 5th May 1980. (See picture 84). Curzon Street No. 1 Box and No. 2 Box were replaced in 1966 by a single one, which lasted until 1989. This was also the lifetime of the new parcels depot.

71.   This fascinating postcard shows the east end of the station in about 1930, with the GWR lines lower centre. They pass over the LMS main lines, beyond the lower border. The two roofs of New Street station are separated by a flat section spanning the taxi road, called Queens Drive. The location was the hub of the tramway system, which lasted until 1953. The left side of the station had been used by the MR and the other by the LNWR. It became a joint station in 1897. (P.Laming coll.)

72.   Standing at the east end on 21st May 1948 is class 2P 4-4-0 no. 511, soon to become 40511. Behind it is No. 4 Box, which had 73 levers and controlled the west end of the ex-MR side of the station. The former LNWR side had its roof severely damaged by bombing and it was replaced by flat canopies. (H.C.Casserley)

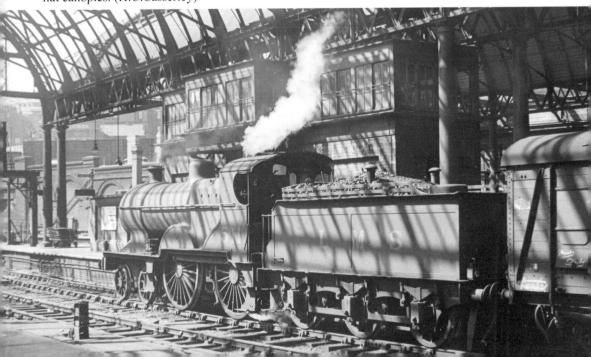

73.   The other side of No. 4 Box is above the tender of class 2P 4-4-0 no. 40486 on 26th May 1951. The fine train shed had been completed in 1885, but all would be lost in the early 1960s. Demolition of the MR section began in April 1964 and the LNWR part in December 1965, this including the Queens Hotel. (H.C.Casserley)

74.   Here is the scene of chaos on 22nd April 1965 as the footbridge over Queens Drive is exposed. In the background are some of the post-war platform canopies. Most of the work was completed in time for some electric services to begin on 5th December 1966. The new concrete building had unpopular low headroom on the platforms and elsewhere. By 1995 the station was taking up to 630 trains per day. (B.W.L.Brooksbank)

75. A rare view from a 24th floor in April 2004 features the crossroads over the western approaches and the recent additional covered footbridge, with four bay windows. The structure was a fire safety requirement. A total rebuild of the station began in 2013 and the car park lost alternate floors, 10 tonne blocks of concrete being cut out. Lorries moved away over 7000 tonnes. (M.J.Stretton)

Lichfield → Birmingham → Longbridge and Redditch

		SX	SO				SX		SO	SX	SO	SX	SO	SX	SX	SX		SO	SX	SO	SX	SX
Lichfield Trent Valley	d			06 08		06 38	06 53				07 09	07 18	07 24		07 34				07 39	07 47	07 53		
Lichfield City	d			06 12		06 42	06 57		07 13	07 13	07 22	07 27		07 37				07 42	07 50	07 57		08 06
Shenstone	d			06 17		06 47	07 02		07 17	07 17	07 27	07 32		07 42				07 47	07 55	08 01		08 10
Blake Street	d		06 07	06 21	06 37	06 51	07 06	07 07	07 22	07 22	07 31	07 36		07 46				07 51	07 59	08 06		08 15
Butlers Lane	d		06 09	06 24	06 39	06 54	07 09	07 09	07 24	07 24	07 34	07 39		07 49				07 54	08 02	08 08		08 17
Four Oaks	d		06 12	06 26	06 42	06 56	07 11	07 12	07 27	07 27	07 36	07 41	07 42	07 51	07 56			07 56	08 04	08 11	08 11	08 20
Sutton Coldfield	d		06 15	06 29	06 44	06 59	07 14	07 14	07 29	07 29	07 39	07 44	07 44	07 54	07 59			07 59	08 07	08 14	08 14	08 23
Wylde Green	d		06 18	06 32	06 47	07 02	07 17	07 17	07 32	07 32	07 42	07 47	07 47	07 57	08 02			08 02	08 10	08 17	08 17	08 26
Chester Road	d		06 19	06 34	06 49	07 04	07 19	07 19	07 34	07 34		07 49	07 49		08 03			08 03		08 18	08 18	
Erdington	d		06 21	06 35	06 50	07 05	07 20	07 20	07 35	07 35		07 50	07 50		08 05			08 05		08 20	08 20	
Gravelly Hill	d		06 23	06 38	06 53	07 08	07 23	07 23	07 38	07 38		07 53	07 53		08 07			08 07		08 22	08 22	
Aston	70 d		06 26	06 41	06 56	07 11	07 26	07 26	07 41	07 41	08 07	07 56	07 56	08 03	08 10			08 10	08 16	08 25	08 25	08 32
Duddeston	70 d		06 29	06 43	06 58	07 13	07 28	07 28	07 43	07 43		07 58	07 58		08 13			08 13		08 28	08 28	
Birmingham New Street	70 a		06 33	06 47	07 02	07 17	07 32	07 32	07 47	07 47	08 02	08 02	08 02	08 08	08 17			08 17	08 24	08 32	08 32	08 37
	d	06 05	06 20	06 35	06 35	06 50	07 05	07 20	07 35	07 35	07 50	07 50	07 55	08 04	08 04	08 10	06 19	08 20	08 33	08 35	08 36	08 40
Five Ways	d	06 08	06 23	06 38	06 38	06 53	07 08	07 23	07 38	07 38	07 53	07 53	07 58	08 07	08 07	08 13	06 22	08 23	08 36	08 38	08 39	08 43
University	d	06 12	06 27	06 42	06 42	06 57	07 12	07 27	07 42	07 42	07 57	07 57	08 02	08 11	08 11	08 17	06 26	08 27	08 40	08 42	08 43	08 47
Selly Oak	d	06 14	06 29	06 44	06 44	06 59	07 14	07 29	07 44	07 44	07 59	07 59	08 04	08 13	08 13	08 18	06 29		08 44	08 45	08 49	
Bournville	d	06 16	06 31	06 46	06 46	07 01	07 16	07 31	07 46	07 46	08 01	08 01	08 06	08 15	08 15	08 21	06 31		08 46	08 47	08 51	
Kings Norton	d	06 19	06 34	06 49	06 49	07 04	07 19	07 34	07 49	07 49	08 04	08 04	08 09	08 18	08 18	08 24	06 33	08 34	08 49	08 50	08 54	
Northfield	d	06 22	06 37	06 52	06 52	07 07	07 22	07 37	07 52	07 52	08 07	08 07	08 12	08 21	08 21	08 27	06 36	08 37	08 52	08 53	08 57	
Longbridge	d	06 24	06 28 a	06 39	06 54	06 58	07 09 a	07 24	07 27 a	07 39	07 58	08 06 a	08 09 a	08 09 a	08 14	08 28	06 38	08 23	08 26 a	08 29 a	08 38	08 54	08 54
Barnt Green	d	06 36		07 06	07	07 36		08 06			08	08 36	08 36							09 06	09		
Alvechurch	d	06 41		07 11	07 11	07 41		08 11		08 11		08 41	08 41							09 11	09 11		
Redditch	a	06 46		07 16	07 16	07 46		08 16		08 16		08 46	08 46							09 16	09 16		

Electric traction began on the route on 12th July 1993 and most trains terminated at Lichfield Trent Valley thereon. The early morning service is on offer. There were two trains per hour over the entire route.

BIRMINGHAM
CURZON STREET

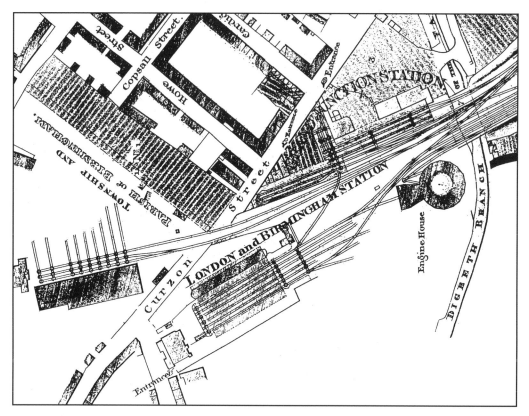

XXI. The 1839 map shows that the L&BR terminal roads are each fitted with three small turntables, as are three of those at the GJR terminus above it. On the right is a branch of the Fazeley Canal and the goods depot is on the left. The street pattern has subsequently changed completely.

Diagrams and other views can be seen in the *Birmingham to Wolverhampton* ***and*** *Bromsgrove to Birmingham* ***albums in this series.***

This extract from May 1974 shows mainly morning services and that
a regular pattern operated from that time. There were no Sunday trains.

Birmingham and Walsall

Miles																					
0	Birmingham New Street	68 d	06 10	06 40	07 10	..	07 40	08 10	08 40	..	09 26	09 56	10 26	..	10 56	11 26	11 56	..	12 26	12 56	13 26
1¼	Duddeston	68 d	06 15	06 45	07 15	....	07 45	08 15	08 45	....	..	10 01	....	..	11 01	....	12 01	....	..	13 01	....
2¼	Aston	68 d	06 17	06 47	07 17	....	07 47	08 17	08 47	....	..	10 03	..	..	11 03	..	12 03	..	..	13 03	..
3¼	Witton	d	06 19	06 49	07 19	....	07 49	08 19	08 49	....	..	10 05	..	..	11 05	..	12 05	..	..	13 05	..
4¼	Perry Barr	d	06 22	06 52	07 22	....	07 52	08 22	08 52	....	..	10 08	..	..	11 08	..	12 08	..	..	13 08	..
6	Hamstead	d	06 24	06 54	07 24	....	07 54	08 24	08 54	09 37	10 10	10 37	....	11 10	11 37	12 10	..	12 37	13 10	13 37
9½	Bescot	d	06 30	07 00	07 30	....	08 00	08 30	09 00	09 43	10 16	10 43	....	11 16	11 43	12 16	..	12 43	13 16	13 43
11¼	Walsall	a	06 34	07 04	07 34	....	08 04	08 34	09 04	09 47	10 20	10 47	....	11 20	11 47	12 20	..	12 47	13 20	13 47

76.   The photographer's 1934 Austin 10 is evident in this view of the L&BR terminus, which still stands. It is marked "Entrance" on the map and has Listed status now. (H.C.Casserley)

77.   These are the platforms used for excursion traffic to and from Sutton Coldfield and Sutton Park. They had been opened in the 1870s and closed on 7th May 1893. In later years they were used for fish traffic. They are seen in February 1932. Goods traffic ceased in 1966. (NRM)

DUDDESTON

XXII.   Our route is across the top left area and the station entrance is from Duddeston Mill Road. The two island platforms are flanked by large workshops. Running to the top right corner is the former MR route to Derby. Its terminus was lower left until 1851, when it became Lawley Street Goods Depot. The line to Rugby is on the right and the ex-MR line to Kings Norton is at the bottom of this 1946 map at approximately 3ins to 1 mile.

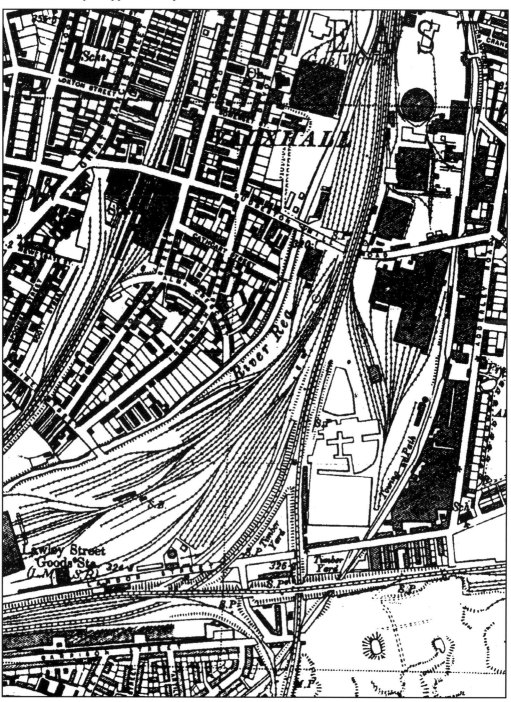

78. This fine view looking northwards towards Aston is from the up slow platform. The station buildings can be seen above the platforms. The station was originally named Vauxhall and became Vauxhall & Duddeston in 1889. It was again renamed on 6th May 1974, becoming Duddeston. To the west side of the station was the original Grand Junction Railway engine shed. This was later converted into a wagon repair depot. The station was rebuilt twice. The building on the right was the up carriage shed until 20th December 1985. (D.J.Norton/M.Norton)

79. This is the post-war rebuild style. Ex-LNWR class 7F "Super D" no. 48930 hauls the SLS special northwards on 2nd June 1962. (R.Shenton)

80. The class 323 EMUs were introduced in 1995 and no. 323206 is seen on 1st May 2009. Quadrupling here and northwards took place in 1891. The tracks were still in place at the left island platform, but were little used since the shed on the left had ceased to serve for maintenance of engineering equipment. It had started life as the GJR engine shed in 1840. (J.Whitehouse)

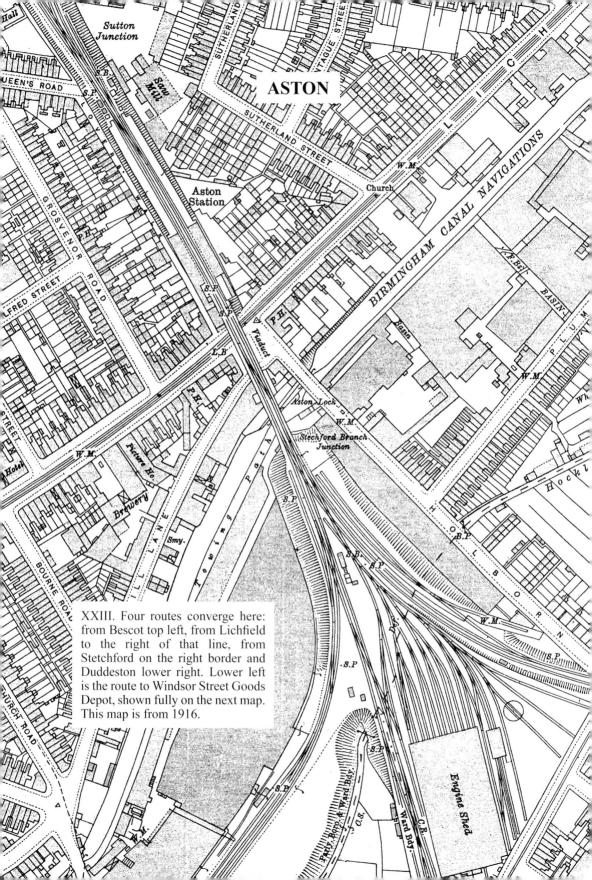

Sutton
Junction

S.B.

S.P.

Saw
Mill

SUTHERLAND

STREET

MONTAGUE STREET

ASTON

QUEEN'S ROAD

Hall

GROSVENOR ROAD

SUTHERLAND STREET

Aston
Station

P.H.

W.M.

Church

L I C H F

BIRMINGHAM CANAL NAVIGATIONS

F. Bsn.

BASIN

P.L.U.M.

S.P.

S.P.

L.B.

P.H.

Viaduct

P.H.

Basin

W.M.

Aston Lock

W.M.

Stechford Branch
Junction

Wh.

W.M.

Towing Path

S.P.

H.O.L.B.O.R.N

O.B.P.

Hock.l.

ALFRED STREET

STREET

Hotel

W.M.

Picture Ho.

Brewery

WELL LANE

Smy.

S.B.

S.P.

W.M.

S.P.

XXIII. Four routes converge here:
from Bescot top left, from Lichfield
to the right of that line, from
Stetchford on the right border and
Duddeston lower right. Lower left
is the route to Windsor Street Goods
Depot, shown fully on the next map.
This map is from 1916.

BOURNE ROAD

CHURCH ROAD

S.P.

S.P.

S.P.

S.P.

Parly. Boro. & Ward Bdy.

C.S.

Ward Bdy.

C.B.

Engine Shed

W.M.

81.   This view is southwestwards and the signals on the right are for goods trains bound for Windsor Street Depot. The station opened in November 1854 and was rebuilt in 1993. (P.Laming coll.)

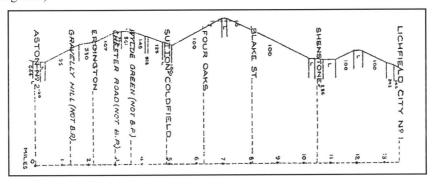

82.   The locomotive depot was coded 3D when these two photographs were taken in about 1950. In 1960 to 1963 it was 21D and 2J until closure in 1965. This is the coaling plant. (R.S.Carpenter coll.)

83. A view towards the station has the Stetchford lines on the right and the signals for the Duddeston route on the left. There was an allocation of 53 locomotives in 1945. (R.S.Carpenter coll.)

84. This general view of the frontage to Windsor Street Goods Depot is from the 1970s. In the 1960s this Goods Depot was the starting point for a "Condor" train between Birmngham and Glasgow. The double track branch from Aston, which served the goods yard and the adjacent gas works, was electrified as part of the West Midland area electrification scheme in 1967. The rail traffic to the gas works ceased in 1974 and the goods yard closed on 12th May 1980, when the remaining traffic was transferred to Lawley Street and Wednesbury Steel Terminal. The track was lifted in September of the same year. (M.Hollick coll.)

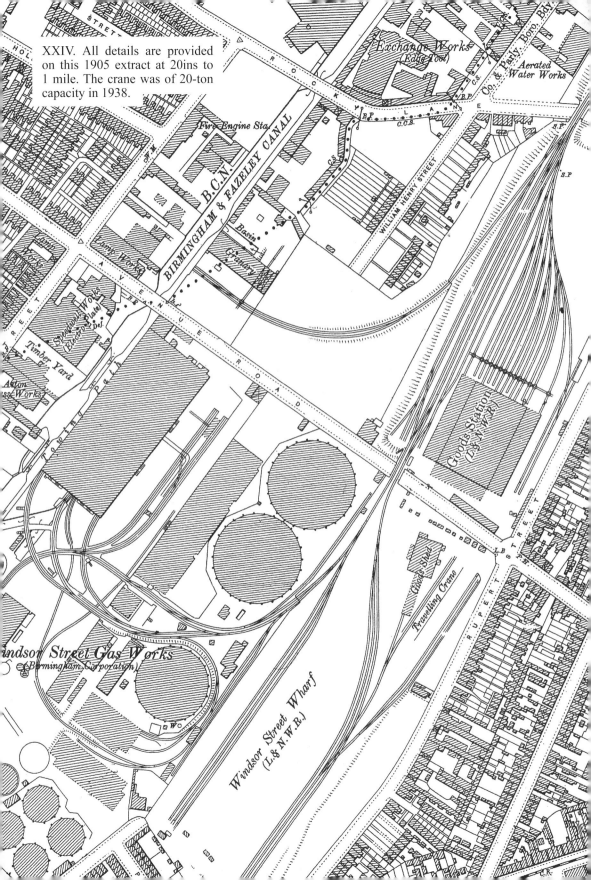

XXIV. All details are provided on this 1905 extract at 20ins to 1 mile. The crane was of 20-ton capacity in 1938.

Exchange Works
(Edge Tool)

Aerated Water Works

Fire Engine Sta.

B.C.N.

BIRMINGHAM & FAZELEY CANAL

Basin

Graving

WILLIAM HENRY STREET

Lamp Works

AVENUE ROAD

Speedwell Works
Electric Bty.

Timber Yard

Aston
ss Works

Fowling Path

Goods Station
(L. & N.W.R.)

Goods Shed

Travelling Crane

RUPERT STREET

Windsor Street Gas Works
(Birmingham Corporation)

Windsor Street Wharf
(L. & N.W.R.)

85.   A DMU working a Cross City service is seen in 1985. Both Aston signal boxes were closed on 4th July 1966, when the New Street power box came into use. (J.Whitehouse)

86.   Entering from the north in September 1985 is a class 47 with container wagons running from Coatbridge to Southampton. It is arriving from Bescot. (J.Whitehouse)

GRAVELLY HILL

XXV. This 1915 edition includes a signal box, which does not appear in the photographs. The dwellings are mostly semi-detached near the station, which would have justified the term "middle class" in that era.

87. The setting sun brought ideal lighting of the main buildings in this postcard view. The cutting continues northwards for around half a mile. (P.Laming coll.)

88.   A record from 3rd March 1984 shows that the view in the other direction was similar. The down platform would take eight coaches and the up seven in 2013. (A.Price/Colour-Rail.com)

ERDINGTON

XXVI. The 1915 edition shows predominantly terraces and that the station was rather remote from the goods yard. This has sunken roads ideal for unloading and storing coal. A 5-ton crane was provided later; the yard closed on 10th August 1964.

89. All structures are made of timber to minimise settlement on the embankment. The sign advises "Wait here for Third Class". Returnable wicker baskets were used widely for a range of merchandise. (P.Laming coll.)

90. Sadly undated, this photograph is a link with the past, with boarded buildings and gas lamps. The signals probably still had oil lamps with wicks that needed weekly trimming. (SLS coll.)

91. Smart new buildings appeared at the time of electrification, together with new indicators. The one on the left advises that the 15.38 to Lichfield is on time. No. 323216 is arriving on 24th August 2009. Both platforms could take ten cars. (J.Whitehouse)

CHESTER ROAD

SHEFFIELD ROAD

Schools

F.B.

S.Ps.

YEWTR

Anstey College

MARSTON ROAD

LIME GROVE

F.P.

M.P

Tk.

CHESTER

Chester Road
Station

Bowling
Green

L.B.

Chester
Villa

Tank

S.P.

Def.

ROAD

FLORENCE ROA

BROADFIELDS

B.P

4ft.R.H.

Def.

4ft.R.H.

B.P.

B.P.

B.P.

Def.

XXVII. The 1915 extract shows the largest houses to be closest to the station and that the line passes over Old Chester Road. This was numbered A452 in 1919. The small goods yard closed on 17th November 1958.

92. We are looking north on 3rd October 1965 and can spot a small ticket window conveniently close to the gate. Gas lighting was still in use. There had been a ground frame on the platform to work the siding points until 20th March 1960. (R.M.Casserley coll.)

93. The station was opened on 1st December 1863 and was photographed on 3rd March 1968. The building on the left was later dismantled and moved to Market Bosworth on the Battlefield Line. (D.Bathurst)

94. No. 323212 was recorded at 10.16 on 9th May 2012. Shelters of a different style were provided here prior to electrification and they gave better weather protection than previously. (J.Whitehouse)

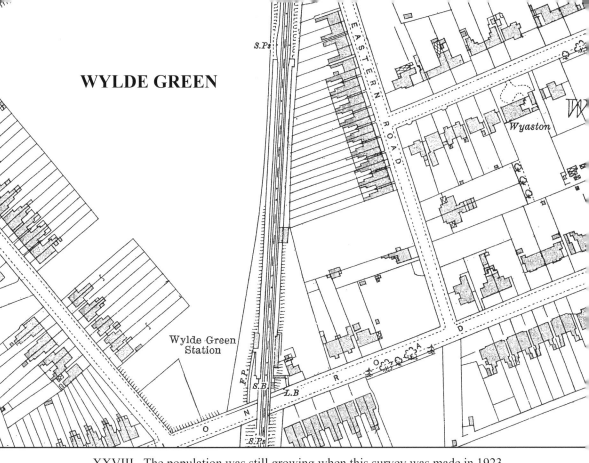

WYLDE GREEN

XXVIII. The population was still growing when this survey was made in 1923.

95.   The standard layout of buildings and signs was replicated here, as seen on a classic postcard reproduction. Again, third class passengers were told their place. (P.Laming coll.)

96.   The box acted as a block post and is shown on the map, but the closure date is not known. The crossing was for staff and parcel traffic. (Lens of Sutton Association)

97.   The entrance to the footpath to the station is included in this view from the 1970s. A Park & Ride plan came in 1970 and 45 cars could be parked. (M.Westley/Warwickshire Railways)

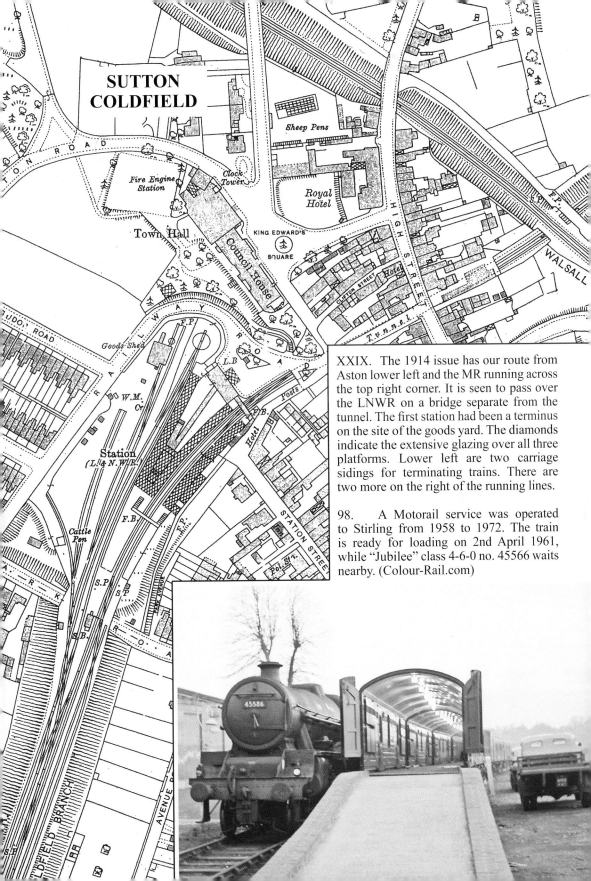

SUTTON COLDFIELD

Sheep Pens

Fire Engine Station

Clock Tower

Royal Hotel

Town Hall

KING EDWARD'S SQUARE

Council House

Goods Shed

L.B

W.M.Cr

Posts

F.B

Hotel

Station (L.& N.W.R.)

F.B

F.P.

Cattle Pen

S.P.

S.B.

XXIX. The 1914 issue has our route from Aston lower left and the MR running across the top right corner. It is seen to pass over the LNWR on a bridge separate from the tunnel. The first station had been a terminus on the site of the goods yard. The diamonds indicate the extensive glazing over all three platforms. Lower left are two carriage sidings for terminating trains. There are two more on the right of the running lines.

98.   A Motorail service was operated to Stirling from 1958 to 1972. The train is ready for loading on 2nd April 1961, while "Jubilee" class 4-6-0 no. 45566 waits nearby. (Colour-Rail.com)

99. Massive cranes had been on site on 23rd January 1955 following the derailment of the 12.15pm York to Bristol 10-coach train, hauled by class 5 4-6-0 no. 45274. It was being driven by a pilotman due to diversions. He and 14 passengers lost their lives, due to excessive speed. This crane is just on bridge renewal work on 2nd September 1962. (Colour-Rail.com)

100. The prospective passenger's perspective was particularly pleasurable. The front was faithfully photographed in February 1965. (Lens of Sutton Association)

101. DMU no. T318 is bound for Lichfield City and is about to enter the 173yd long tunnel. On the left is the roof over the path down from the booking hall to two of the platforms. (J.Whitehouse)

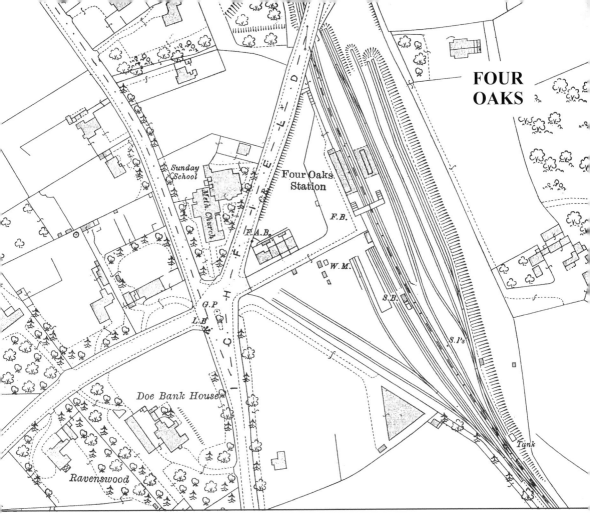

FOUR OAKS

Sunday School

Meth. Church

Four Oaks Station

F.B.

F.A.B.

W.M.

S.B.

G.P

L.B

S.I's

Doe Bank House

Tank

Ravenswood

XXX. The 1914 edition has the Methodist Church in the prime position, for the benefit of all. The two sidings near the left boundary and the four on the right were mainly used for carriage berthing.

102.   Many trains serving the suburbs terminated here, the bay platform being on the left in this southward view. The massive ventilators are over the facilities for gentlemen. (P .Laming coll.)

103.   The frontage of Four Oaks Station is seen in February 1949. The station opened on 15th December 1884 with the extension of the line from Sutton Coldfield to Lichfield City. The down sidings were taken out of use on 1st September 1966. (E.S.Russell)

104.   We look north on 9th July 1955 as class 2P 2-6-4T no. 41224 waits in the bay to return to Longbridge. A wagon of coal is evident in the goods yard, which closed on 7th December 1964. (R.S.Carpenter)

105. A DMU destined for Longbridge is departing not long before the signal box closed on 9th October 1992. The new Aston Signalling Centre then took over. The bay could take eight cars, the other platforms seven . The car park had 250 spaces. (J.Whitehouse)

BIRMINGHAM, MONUMENT LANE, BESCOT, WALSALL, and WOLVERHAMPTON

Week Days

Miles		a.m	a.m	a.m	a.m		a.m	a.m	a.m	a.m	a.m	a.m	p.m	p.m	p.m	a.m	pm
	50 London (Euston)dep	S	12‡2	..	V	TC Stechford dep. 7 15 a.m. to Llandudno arr. 11 50 a.m (Table 50)	..	S	..		N	..	E	S	S	8 55	..
—	**Birmingham** (N.St)dep	..	5 55	6 33	..		7 37		8 35	9 0	9 20	9 45	..	..	..	1215	..
1¼	Vauxhall & Duddeston	..	5 58	6 36	..		7 40	TC to Black'l arr. 12 9 p.m. (Table 50)	..	..	..	9 48	..	..	12 9	1218	..
2¼	Aston	..	6 3	6 40	7 25		7 44		..	..	9 28	9 53	..	..	1212	1222	..
3¼	Witton	..	6 7	6 44	..		7 47		..	..	..	9 56	..	..	1216	1225	..
4¼	Perry Barr	..	6 11	6 47	7 33		7 50		..	9T14	9 37	9 59	..	..	1219	1228	..
—	Monument Lane	..	..	..	..		..		8 39	TC to Blackpool arr. 12 40 p.m. (Table 50)	TC to Morecambe (E. Rd.) (Table 50)	..	..	..	..	..	..
—	Winson Green	..	..	..	..		..		..			..	..	..	..	..	..
5¾	Great Barr **A**	..	6 17	6 51	..		7 54		8 48			10 3	..	..	1223	1232	..
9¼	Bescot	..	6 26	7 0	..		8 3		8 57			1013	..	..	1232	1243	..
11	**Walsall** arr	..	6 30	7 4	..		8 11		9 1			1017	..	..	1236	1247	..
	Walsall dep	6 20	6 57	..	..		8 22	8 38	9 12			..	12 3	1212	..	..	142
—	Bescot	..	..	..	..		..	..	..			..	..	..	..	..	..
—	Pleck	..	6 59	..	..		8 24	8 42	9 14			..	12 5	1214	..	..	144
10¾	Darlaston	6 26	7 2	..	..		8 27	8 47	9 17			..	12 8	1217	..	..	147
12¾	Willenhall (Bilston St)	6 31	7 8	..	..		8 31	8 53	9 21			..	1212	1221	..	..	151
15½	**Wolverhampton**... arr	6 43	7 17	..	8 12		8 40	9 2	9 30		10 0	..	1221	1230	..	..	2 0

Miles		a.m	a.m	a.m	p.m	p.m	p.m	p.m	p.m	p.m	p.m	p.m	p.m	p.m	p.m	p.m	p.m.
	50 London (Euston)dep	1020	1125	1132	..	E	2 15	S	E	..	E	..	S	4 35	5 45	6 55	7 5
—	**Birmingham** (N.St)dep	1 20	2K35	4 12	..	..	5 26	..	..	6 7	..	6 33	..	7 12	8 36	9 25	10u35
1¼	Vauxhall & Duddeston	1 23	2K38	4 15	..	5 14	..	..	5 35	6 10	..	6 36	..	7 15	8 39	9 28	10u38
2¼	Aston	1 27	2K42	4 19	..	5 17	..	..	5 44	6 16	..	6 40	..	7 19	8 43	9 32	10u42
3¼	Witton	1 30	2K45	4 22	..	5 21	..	..	5 48	6 21	..	6 47	..	7 22	8 46	..	..
4¼	Perry Barr	1 33	2K48	4 25	..	5 25	..	..	5 53	6 25	..	6 53	..	7 25	8 49	9 37	10u47
—	Monument Lane	..	..	..	..	..	..	..	..	..	..	..	..	..	..	..	..
—	Winson Green	..	..	..	..	..	..	..	..	..	..	..	..	..	..	..	..
5¾	Great Barr **A**	1 37	2K52	4 29	..	5F29	..	..	5 58	6 29	..	6 57	..	7 29	8 53	9 41	10u51
9¼	Bescot	1 48	3K2	4 39	..	5 38	5 45	..	6 7	6 39	..	7 6	..	7 38	9 3	9 50	11u 1
11	**Walsall** arr	1 52	3K6	4 43	..	5 42	5 49	..	6 11	6 43	..	7 10	..	7 42	9 7	9 54	11u 5
	Walsall dep	..	..	..	5 19	..	..	6 8	..	..	6 44	..	7 30	8 8	..	10 2	..
—	Bescot	..	..	..	..	..	..	..	..	..	..	..	..	..	..	..	..
—	Pleck	..	..	..	5 21	..	..	6 10	..	..	6 48	..	7 34	8 10	..	10 4	..
10¾	Darlaston	..	..	..	5 24	..	..	6 13	..	..	6 52	..	7 37	8 16	..	10 7	..
12¾	Willenhall (Bilston St)	..	..	..	5 30	..	..	6 17	..	..	6 57	..	7 41	8 21	..	1011	..
15½	**Wolverhampton**... arr	..	..	..	5 39	..	..	6 26	..	..	7 6	..	7 50	8 30	..	1020	..

June 1950

Sundays

	a.m	a.m	a.m	p.m	p.m	p.m	p.m	p.m
Wolverhampton........dep	..	9 30	11 7	1 28	..	..	..	1015
Willenhall (Bilston St)...	..	..	..	..	..	..	..	..
Darlaston	..	..	..	..	..	..	..	..
Pleck	..	..	..	..	..	..	..	..
Bescot	..	..	..	..	..	..	..	..
Walsall arr	..	9 48	1123	1 44	..	..	..	1031
Walsall dep	9 5	..	1 30	3 10	4 10	7 25	9 32	..
Bescot	9 9	..	1 34	3 14	4 14	7 30	9 36	..
Great Barr **A**	9 15	..	1 40	3 20	4 20	7 37	9 42	..
Winson Green	..	..	..	..	..	..	..	..
Monument Lane	..	..	..	..	..	..	..	..
Perry Barr	9 19	..	1 44	3 24	4 24	7 42	9 46	..
Witton	..	..	..	..	..	..	..	..
Aston	9 24	..	1 49	3 29	4 29	7 47	9 51	..
Vauxhall & Duddeston....	9 31	..	1 55	3 36	4 36	7 56	9 58	..
Birmingham (N.St.)....arr	9 36	..	2 0	3 41	4 41	8 3	10 3	..
59 London (Euston).....arr	1 35	..	5 15	..	7 50	..	..	..

A Station for (2 miles from Great Barr)
A 3 minutes *earlier* on Sats
B Sats. only. Runs 29th July to 9th September inclusive
E or E Except Saturdays
F Fridays only
J Sats. only. Runs 1st July to 22nd July inclusive
J Sunday mornings only
K 5 minutes later on Sats.
N Sats. only. Runs to 9th September inclusive
N 2 minutes later on Sats.
P Change at Vauxhall
S Saturdays only
T Stops to take up only
TC Through Carriages

BUTLERS LANE

106.   A 1962 panorama reveals the extensive housing developments which had recently taken place. An experimental halt was opened on 30th September 1957. It was so successful that it remained open and "Halt" dropped from the name in April 1963. (B.W.L.Brooksbank)

107.   Trains ceased to call from 20th October 1991 until 23rd September 1992, while the platforms were rebuilt and new accommodation provided. No. 323206 runs south on 27th August 2013. (Colour-Rail.com)

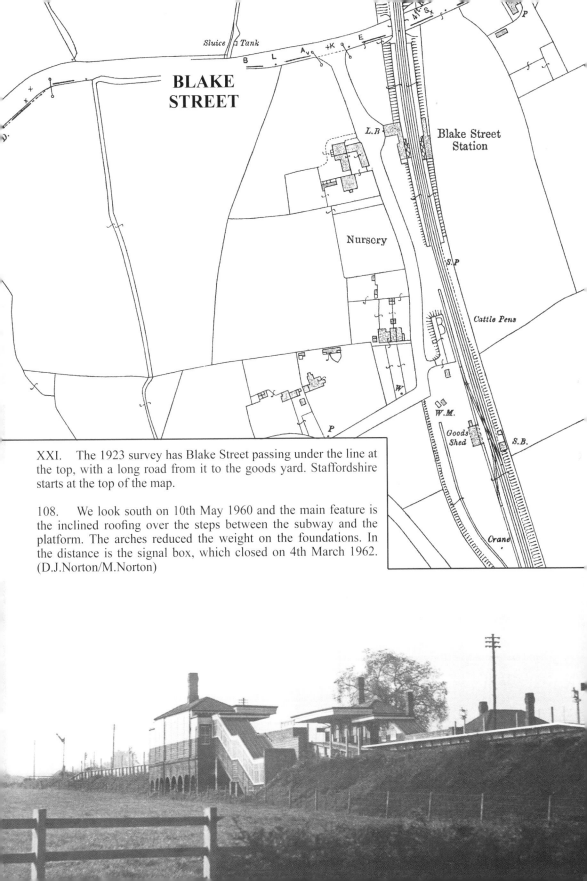

BLAKE STREET

Sluice □ *Tank*

B L A +K E

L.B

Blake Street Station

Nursery

S.P

Cattle Pens

W.

W.M.

Goods Shed   S.B.

P.

Crane

XXI.   The 1923 survey has Blake Street passing under the line at the top, with a long road from it to the goods yard. Staffordshire starts at the top of the map.

108.   We look south on 10th May 1960 and the main feature is the inclined roofing over the steps between the subway and the platform. The arches reduced the weight on the foundations. In the distance is the signal box, which closed on 4th March 1962. (D.J.Norton/M.Norton)

109.　　The station is at the northern edge of the urban area and some peak hour trains have for long turned back here. The goods yard closed on 7th December 1964. There were two ground frames in place from 1962 to 1965. There is a permanent red signal at the north end of the up platform. (J.Whitehouse)

　　　　The May 1998 service for mid-afternoon indicates the basic pattern since that time, when through running to Stafford was restored. Sunday trains became hourly, Tame Bridge Parkway had a service from London Marylebone between 28th April 2008 and 28th January 2011. There were four trains, weekdays only, initially, this soon being reduced to three.

Birmingham and Wolverhampton
Rugeley and Stafford

Station	CT SX B	CT	CT	CT C		CT	CT	CT	CT	CT C		CT B	CT C	CT SX C	CT SO	CT SX		CT SO
Birmingham New Street 🚉 .... 68, 69 d	15 12	15 30	....	15 42	....	16 00	16 12	....	16 30	16 42	....	17 00	....	17 09	17 12	17 27	....	17 30
Duddeston . . . . 69 d	15 16	.	.	15 46	....	.	16 16	.	.	16 47	.	.	.	17 13	17 16	.	.	.
Aston . . . . 69 d	15 19	.	.	15 48	....	.	16 18	.	.	16 49	.	.	.	17 15	17 18	.	....	17 34
Witton . . . . . . d	15 21	.	.	15 50	....	.	16 20	.	.	16 52	.	.	.	17 17	17 20	.	....	17 38
Perry Barr . . . . d	15 23	....	.	15 53	....	.	16 22	.	.	16 54	.	.	.	17 20	17 22	.	.	.
Hamstead . . . . d	15 26	.	.	15 55	....	.	16 25	.	.	16 58	.	.	.	17 22	17 25	.	.	.
Tame Bridge Park Way . d	15 31	15 45	.	15 59	....	16 17	16 28	.	16 45	17 02	.	17 15	....	17 26	17 28	17 39	....	17 45
Bescot Stadium . . . d	15 33	.	.	16 02	....	.	16 31	.	.	17 04	.	.	.	17 29	17 31	.	....	17 48
Wolverhampton . . . . . 68 d	....	.	15 47	....	.	.	16 28	.	.	17 12	.	.	.	.	.	.	.	.
Walsall . . . . a	15 37	15 51	15 59	16 06	.	16 22	16 38	16 40	16 51	17 08	.	17 20	17 24	17 33	17 35	17 45	....	17 51
. . . . d	15 37	....	.	.	.	16 23	.	.	.	.	.	17 21	.	.	.	17 45	.	17 52
Bloxwich . . . . . d	15 44	.	.	.	.	16 30	.	.	.	.	.	17 28	.	.	.	17 52	.	17 59
Bloxwich North . . . . d	15 46	.	.	.	.	16 32	.	.	.	.	.	17 30	.	.	.	17 54	.	18 01
Landywood . . . . d	15 50	.	.	.	.	16 36	.	.	.	.	.	17 34	.	.	.	17 58	.	18 05
Cannock . . . . . d	15 54	.	.	.	.	16 41	.	.	.	.	.	17 38	.	.	.	18 03	.	18 09
Hednesford . . . . d	15 59	.	.	.	.	16 46	.	.	.	.	.	17 43	.	.	.	18 00	.	18 14
Rugeley Town . . . . d	16 22	.	.	.	.	16 54	.	.	.	.	.	17 51	.	.	.	18a15	.	18a21
Rugeley Trent Valley . . 67 d	16 25	.	.	.	.	16 57	.	.	.	.	.	18 00	.	.	.	.	.	.
Stafford . . . . . . 67, 68 a	16 39	.	.	.	.	17 10	.	.	.	.	.	18 12	.	.	.	.	.	.

B　From Stafford
C　From Walsall

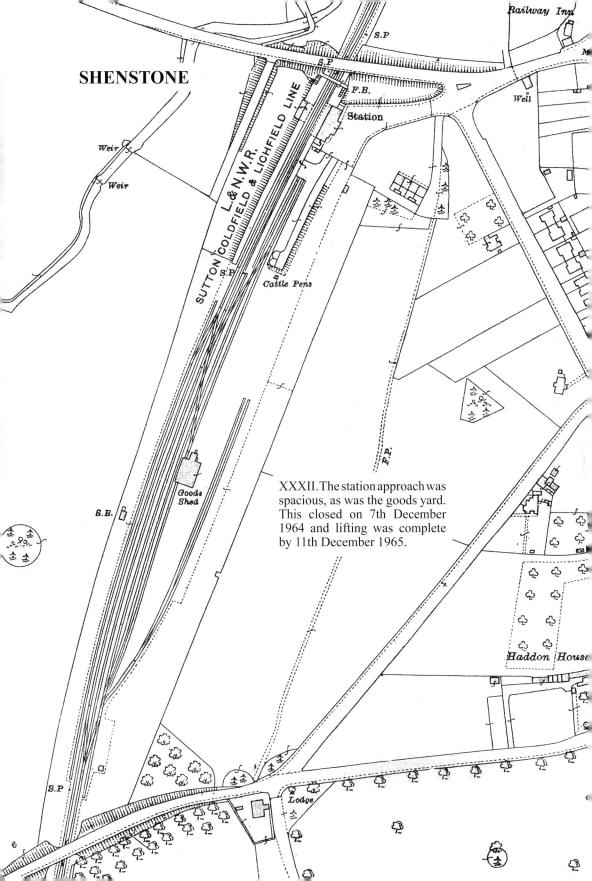

SHENSTONE

Railway Inn

S.P

S.P

F.B.

Station

Well

L. & N.W.R.

SUTTON COLDFIELD & LICHFIELD LINE

Weir

Weir

S.P

Cattle Pens

F.P.

XXXII. The station approach was spacious, as was the goods yard. This closed on 7th December 1964 and lifting was complete by 11th December 1965.

Goods Shed

S.B.

Haddon House

S.P

Lodge

110. The east elevation is seen in about 1959, with the fine collection of stylish chimneys. Intricate tracery can be enjoyed between the canopy stanchions. The up building was still standing in 2013. (R.S.Carpenter)

111. The platform canopies are of note in that they have no stanchions, a common feature of GWR stations. The population rose from 1865 in 1901 to 5174 in 1961. (W.A.Camwell/SLS)

112. The signal box can be found on the map; it closed on 31st May 1970. Nearest to it is a refuge siding. Since the advent of clockface timetables, only alternate trains have generally stopped here. (R.S.Carpenter)

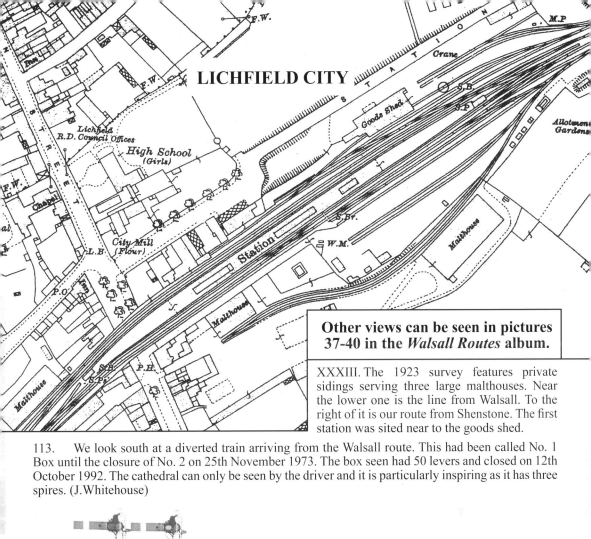

LICHFIELD CITY

Other views can be seen in pictures 37-40 in the *Walsall Routes* album.

XXXIII. The 1923 survey features private sidings serving three large malthouses. Near the lower one is the line from Walsall. To the right of it is our route from Shenstone. The first station was sited near to the goods shed.

113.   We look south at a diverted train arriving from the Walsall route. This had been called No. 1 Box until the closure of No. 2 on 25th November 1973. The box seen had 50 levers and closed on 12th October 1992. The cathedral can only be seen by the driver and it is particularly inspiring as it has three spires. (J.Whitehouse)

114. This is the view south looking towards the site of No. 2 Box in the late 1980s. The disused goods shed is on the right and the roof of the main station building is above the fifth coach of this diverted train. (J.Whitehouse)

115. No. 323205 is northbound and has stopped just beyond the canopy. This platform takes seven coaches, while the up one can welcome eleven. The upper part of the signal is used for access to the single electrified berthing siding. (J.Whitehouse)

116. The exterior was recorded on 17th March 2009. There had been no local passenger trains north hereof between 18th January 1965 and 28th November 1988, when alternate trains began to run to Lichfield Trent Valley. (I.Pell)

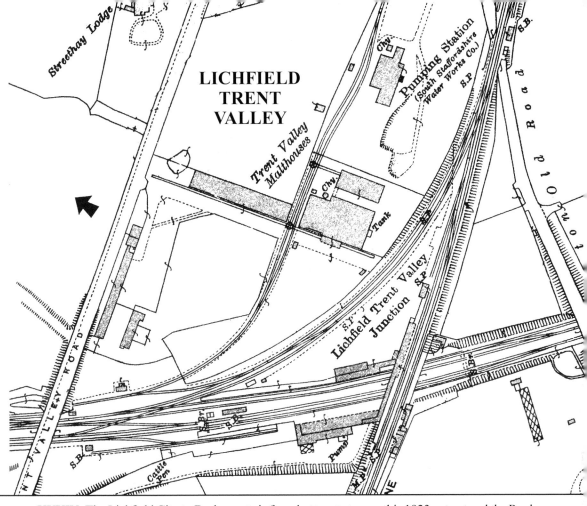

XXXIV. The Lichfield City to Derby route is from bottom to top on this 1923 extract and the Rugby to Stafford line is from right to left.

117.   We are at the high level platforms, looking towards Derby on 23rd March 1957. They were unused from 18th January 1965 until 28th November 1988, by which time they were replaced with concrete structures. (R.M.Casserley)

118.   This panorama from June 1960 has our route across the background and a curve on the left connecting it to the main lines. No. 1 Box is centre; it had 80 levers and was in use until 29th May 2008. (W.A.Camwell/SLS)

The journey from Redditch and Birmingham can be enjoyed with the driver in 1995 by watching the DVD named *Cross City Birmingham*. It is available from Middleton Press.

This location is also featured in the *Rugby to Stafford* and *Walsall Routes* albums from Middleton Press.

119.   We are in High Level Junction Box on 1st April 1986, as no. 45012 climbs up the chord with empty wagons. This box was one of the last LNWR structures to remain in use in 2013. The route to Burton-on-Trent was then almost all double, but was freight only. (N.Allsop)

120.   No. 310102 waits to return to Redditch on 9th August 1993. The new platforms are evident, but the one on the left was not for use by passengers. Alternate trains have generally provided the connections north of Lichfield City. (B.Jennings)

MP Middleton Press
EVOLVING THE ULTIMATE RAIL ENCYCLOPEDIA

Easebourne Lane, Midhurst, West Sussex.
GU29 9AZ   Tel:01730 813169
www.middletonpress.co.uk   email:info@middletonpress.co.uk
A-978 0 906520   B- 978 1 873793   C- 978 1 901706   D-978 1 904474
E- 978 1 906008   F- 978 1 908174

All titles listed below were in print at time of publication - please check current availability by looking at our website - www.middletonpress.co.uk or by requesting a Brochure which includes our LATEST RAILWAY TITLES also our TRAMWAY, TROLLEYBUS, MILITARY and COASTAL series